FINDING MY VOICE

A Journey Into Faith

Joshua Bechtel

Joshua Bechtel
Deut 32:12

PublishAmerica
Baltimore

© 2012 by Joshua Bechtel.
All rights reserved. No part of this book may be reproduced, stored in a retrieval system or transmitted in any form or by any means without the prior written permission of the publishers, except by a reviewer who may quote brief passages in a review to be printed in a newspaper, magazine or journal.

First printing

PublishAmerica has allowed this work to remain exactly as the author intended, verbatim, without editorial input.

Softcover 9781462679485
PUBLISHED BY PUBLISHAMERICA, LLLP
www.publishamerica.com
Baltimore

Printed in the United States of America

Table of Contents

Acknowledgements..............7
Foreword.............................9
Chapter 1..........................12
Chapter 2..........................16
Chapter 3..........................20
Chapter 4..........................24
Chapter 5..........................27
Chapter 6..........................30
Chapter 7..........................35
Chapter 8..........................44
Chapter 9..........................49
Chapter 10........................54
Chapter 11........................71
Chapter 12........................78
Chapter 13........................93
Chapter 14........................99
Chapter 15......................107
Chapter 16......................114
Chapter 17......................118
Chapter 18......................130

Chapter 19............................*138*
Chapter 20............................*146*
Chapter 21............................*151*
Chapter 22............................*155*
Chapter 23............................*166*
Chapter 24............................*176*
Chapter 25............................*181*
Chapter 26............................*200*
Chapter 27............................*206*
Chapter 28............................*211*
Chapter 29............................*219*

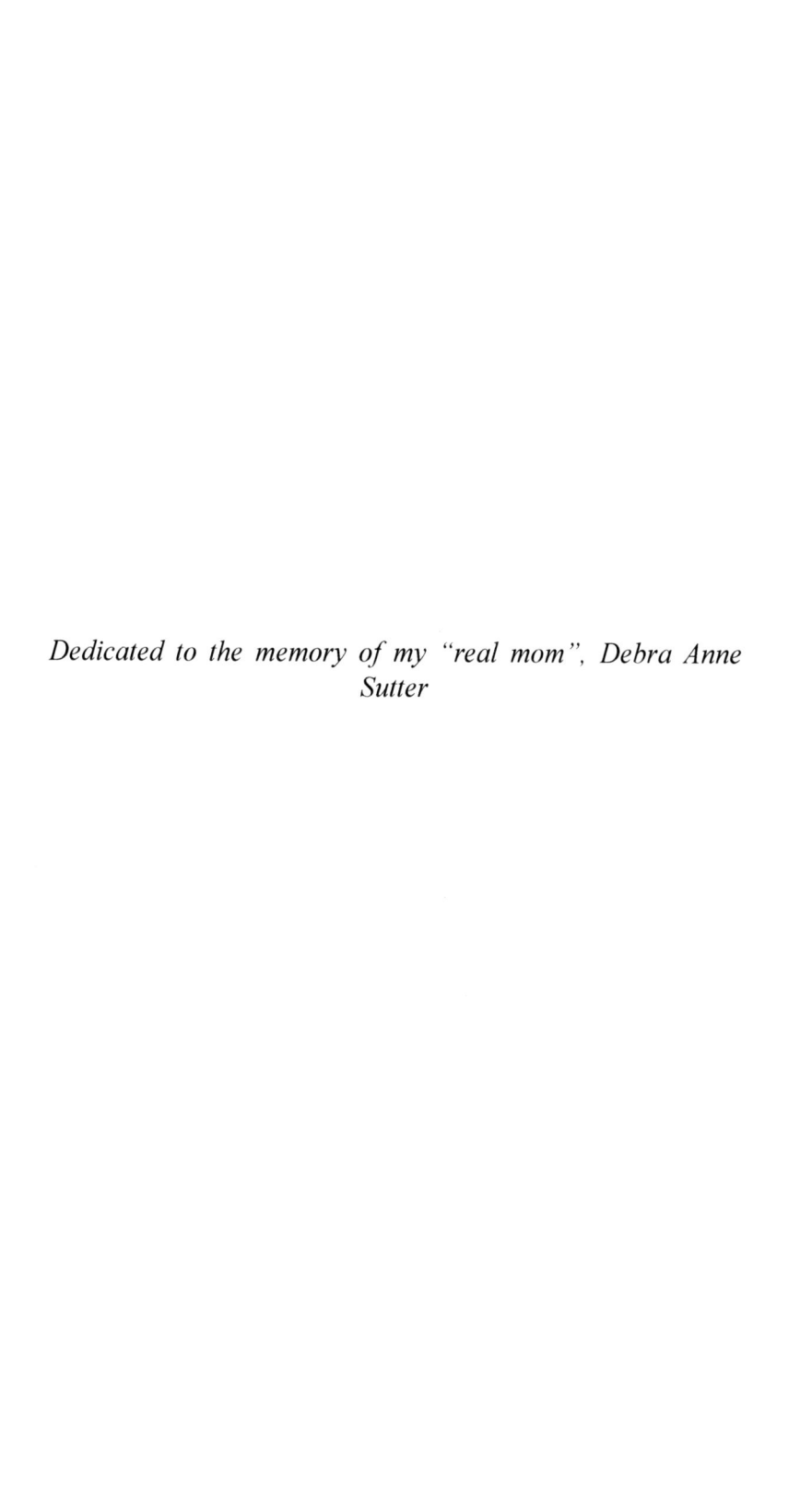

Dedicated to the memory of my "real mom", Debra Anne Sutter

Acknowledgements

This book would not have been written without prodding from a lot of varied people.

Beginning with my *madre adoptiva,* Faythelma Arthel Bechtel. Thanks, too, for being Mom throughout a frankly chaotic childhood and life in general. (I do love you!)

Also, I have had several mentors push me to write this. Among them, Jeremy Sensenig. Thanks for walking with me through some very dark times...and for pointing me, the best you could, to the Light.

Also, my co-staff guys from when I worked at FSTC...truth sometimes takes a while to sink in.

There have been a number of folks who have been kind enough to review and offer feedback on this manuscript during the (several) years it was being written. This includes enduring many and varied "notes" that appeared on Facebook and generated much discussion. You know who you are...and accept my thanks!

I would also like to thank the Rich Perry family for "adopting" me as an honorary Perry. (You guys rock!)

Special thanks to Harvey Yoder for convincing me it was worth my time to keep writing this book. (My spirit still does call you "dad".)

Also, thanks to my Intermediate Sunday School teacher from way back in the day for writing an amazing forward.

Also, thanks to Nate Schlabach for doing the final edit... (three years staring at a manuscript blinds one to the most obvious typos.)

Finally, and most importantly, I thank God, who "alone did lead him"...often when I knew it not. (I have finally found my life verse.)

(Most of the names in the pages that follow are actual. There is one family who's names have been changed per their request.)

Whatever else this book might be, it is definitely not a "tell all"...it *is* a "tell some." I have in these pages related enough of my story and journey to faith to give you an idea what that journey has been like. I have attempted to tell my story with no "claws or teeth." I have not meant to "paint anyone black"... except myself.

Foreword

What is your view of God?

Is He that perfect, righteous, powerful, and demanding Judge of the Old Testament? Is He swift to punish wrong and disobedience with vengeance and wrath? Yes, God is all that but He is so much more. Today, God wants you to see who He is in Jesus Christ.

He is Lord of the New Covenant. He excels in love, joy, peace, long-suffering, gentleness, goodness, faith, meekness, temperance, mercy, and grace. A loving Son and Saviour, Jesus Christ willingly made Himself "common to man", walking among and with the lowly, the destitute, with criminals, and unclean sinners. He lived to teach and show us "the way" to our heavenly Father's love. He confirms that each person is a precious an unique created being. Each is a special individual who God so loves.

Joshua has victoriously discovered this truth and has rightly laid claim to God's grace through Jesus Christ.

Have you ever wondered, WHY you are you?

Read about this young man's amazing discovery and journey to "grace". Have you ever been amazed as you come to discover, and recognize that the Father's love was always there through the lowest valley and darkest nights? There is wisdom in sharing even when it hurts, as Joshua did when he writes: *"God, did I make all that stuff up....about dad?!" "I was sobbing uncontrollably and pounding the floor with my fists as I asked this." "My spirit screams I hate you, God!"*

Yes, often the complexity of life shatters and distorts the love and simplicity of Christ. Who would have ever known this was all about Jesus? Read as Josh expressed in exclamation -*WOW!* This *"is the honest record of a very confusing journey of (into) faith"*. My, how God loves honesty! Truth does not need to change, we do.

Joshua again throws out:*"If I appeared more spiritual, it was a fitting, and perhaps ironic cover up to hide a growing sense of loneliness, self hatred, and subconscious bitterness toward God."* What great stake driving! Read how Jesus Christ set this man's heart free! The mind, the human brain is the most wonderful and advanced computer system ever created. What is imputed through teachings and experience may very well determine the degree of effort needed to counter balance the tug of God within.

In a sense, Josh has spoken for many other people who long for a depth of heart and soul in a cry and search for the heavenly Father's love. I can hear our heavenly Father muse, *Jesus, what will it take to turn this beloved child my direction?* And Jesus might reply with, *Just go easy Father, I can see, feel, and understand the why's… just a little more mercy and I know "grace" will prevail…*

Is it not a "wonder" how God guides us to knowledge of Him, then exercises much patience until we "know" Him? The wonder of wonders is how God Himself being the Holy Spirit within is willing to "dwell", not herd from behind, push along side, nor lead from the front, but "dwell" within…becoming an actual part of every moment, thought, good and bad, while we walk life's journey led by the testimony of His Son, Jesus Christ. God the Holy Spirit inside us, means He understands, means He knows the story more than you or anyone else could attempt to understand. Remember my friend, every person is important, you are individually loved, uniquely different than anyone else, and made in His image, created for His purpose. Luck? you may ask? OK, divine intervention then. Intervention? by whom? Nothing but the blood of Jesus Christ is my reply."*A new commandment I give unto you that ye love one another…"* (John 13:34)

I believe Joshua can say as the Apostle Paul concluded "my grace is sufficient for thee" therefore glorify my son Jesus Christ. Certainly in a conduit of reconciliation, he that refreshes others will himself be refreshed. Thank you Joshua for telling your story and for giving me this opportunity to share in "your story". Your Christian friend and brother in Jesus Christ - Danny Zook :)

Chapter 1

Unanswered, but Answered
The broken toy cannot be fixed
If I don't admit its broken.
Tension and fear won't be resolved
If the differences are not spoken.
This life's a room of broken toys
Of bandaged limbs and cut short joys...
So if I insist on tearless eyes...
When it comes time in paradise
For Him to wipe the tears away
What will He do...
What will I say?
For wine is made by crushing
The grapes we wish were whole...
And gold that has been beaten
Is most beautiful to behold...
No tears in heaven
No sorrows given
We sing as if it brings us joy
But what if
While here on earth
We insist on acted mirth...
If there's no pain
Will there be any depth to our joy?
JPB

I stood in the dead silence of an antique mall somewhere in Indiana. The friends I was with had wandered off to another part of the mall. It dawned on me that they had left me alone, which was okay because I doubt they could have understood what was going through my mind anyway. Maybe I was wrong about that. I tended to assume that people would not be able to understand me and my experiences and what I was thinking. To be honest, I still do....

That's no slight on my friends or anybody else. Its just that I would have had a hard time explaining what was going through my mind. It did not really make sense to me, so how could I hope to explain it to someone else?

Browsing in an antique mall does something to me.

Like what?

It leaves me...depressed ...pensive? ...wistful? I don't know. A little of all of these. None of them really hits it; but then maybe all of them do.

Whatever it was intensified the dull, throbbing migraine I had endured most of that day.

I am not really sure why.

I am in here with some friends...enjoying a Saturday afternoon hopping from one antique mall to another. There is no real reason for this-this lost, empty feeling.

There isn't?

Is it...that distinctive antique shop smell? Or the little old lady at the counter who reminds me suddenly of my real grandma whom I have hardly seen since...

I blinked.

Where on earth did that come from?

I shook myself part way out of my thoughts. And blinked. And blinked again. It slowly sank in what I was looking at: a set of Fisher Price plastic toys called Little People, the ones with bland faces and round flat bottoms that fit in little holes in toy airplanes and houses. They looked old enough to have been new around the time I was young enough to play with them. There was even the "mommie" figure with yellow hair.

Is there a reason the Mom sticks out and not the Dad?

How am I supposed to know?

My mind was racing in so many directions I couldn't keep up with it. Amazing, wistful longings rose up within me. I am grieving for a childhood where my main concern was when the next Dr. Seuss book would be coming out. I sensed the beginnings of a wish as that musty antique store stirred up memories of a childhood that I had tried so hard to forget.

I sensed something flare up in my spirit, questioning God.

I realized that for some reason God would not allow me to forget. Why is such longing, such sadness, such pain evoked in the memory of a toy? I must be teetering toward insanity.

Maybe.

I wish for the childhood that ended when I was two years old.

I knew better than that. I tried to shove the thought away because I was not ready to confront the pain and emotion it would provoke. The thought lingered in my mind. So I allowed it to persist.

I feel like a bundle of confusion. I am glad for the life that I have now. Or, at least, I think I am.

But...is it wrong to wonder what that other life would have been like? Because, honestly, I have wondered...and half wished...a lot.

What about the life I left...that I was taken out of...when I was placed in foster care at 18 months old?

What would have happened if I had not been adopted at 10?

Where would my life have gone if God had not directed it the way He has?

There I was, in a room full of old items that each had an obvious story. Do I have a story, too? And...if I do...is there any sense to it? I felt a violent hunger welling up within me... and a deep, nameless emptiness. I felt something similar to phantom pain that amputees experience after losing a limb... except I could not recall ever having the limb. Maybe my hunger, my longing, my thirst, was intended to drive me...to find GOD?

My quest to find the answer to that question would take me several years of digging back into the crypt of forgotten, almost forbidden memory.

I did not want to, but I knew that I had to.

Chapter 2

*The sky is green
And the grass is blue
At least it seems
That's what life
Taught you;
And you've started
Seeing
You got all your
Life colors wrong...
JPB*

Scattered Photographs and a Ceramic Dish

I was holding a ceramic dish in my hand. It had a picture of a stork with a blanket in its bill. There was a baby in the blanket. There were a couple sprigs of blue flowers and a scroll.

In my great grandmother's handwriting were a few words:

Joshua Paul
8 lbs. 9 ½ oz
November 4
1977.

I know very little about my great grandmother. The main thing I know is what her name was: Idelle Bernier. Aunt Kathy wrote it on an envelope that had a few childhood pictures. She handed me the envelope with some pictures she had salvaged from Grandpa's house after he passed away. I was on a trip out to Oregon when I made a surprise stop at their house on a "5 minute visit" that stretched over an hour.

I held my mom's High School Student Body Card.

Pendleton
High School
Pendleton, Oregon
1973-1974
Student Body Card

There was a logo of a bucking bronco with the words "Let'er Buck" underneath.

I stared at a smiling picture of my mom, when she was 17 or 18. This girl was my mom when she was in High School.

I tried to make sense of all the things I have been told, about those days. I wondered about things that I probably have no right to know.

I am okay with that...I guess.

There are some things I know that I wish I didn't know. Well, I kind of wish I didn't know.

But in a strange way, I am glad I know now.

I looked at another picture. On the back was written "Josh 82" In Grandma Sutter's handwriting.

I was at the end of the walk in front of Grandpa Sutter's. Behind me, a truck with a trailer/canopy on the back. I was wearing blue jeans and a yellow long sleeved pull over. My hair was curly and just a little bit on the long side. The pictures surprised me, and it wasn't the just-a-little-bit-too-long hair.

I do not remember being as happy as I appear on these pictures.

What I saw made me smile a little, and made me want to cry a little.

Am I jaded? I am not sure...how can I be sure? Couldn't I have handled knowing the huge gap between what seemed to be and what actually was?

Maybe I wasn't supposed to know, until not so long ago how loved, missed and wondered about I was.

Maybe, or maybe I could not have handled knowing it? Is there any way of knowing...now? Is there any point in allowing myself to ask the question?

Will I ever know?

With a sigh, I picked up another picture. Joshua Age 5 1982-83 It was an end of the school year picture. I was in Head Start or Kindergarten. Same curly hair. And a mischievous smile. This time I had on a plaid McGregor button up shirt over top a white tee shirt.

Photographs.

A ceramic dish.

Great Grandma made the ceramic dish, painted it, and wrote my name on it, around the time I was born. I knew none of this until Aunt Kathy put it in my hands, along with the pictures, when I was in my early thirties. I don't remember her, or a lot of people who were big when I was small.

The ceramic dish is one of the few links I have to my childhood. I had a few photos, some that were given to me when I was younger. I have gathered other pictures over time on various trips back to Pendleton. And I also have a scrapbook that was begun when I was too young to really understand what it was all about.

There are a lot of tidbits that I have been told along the way.

Memories...remembered. Memories that I willed myself to forget.

A life that I have not understood but have attempted to survive.

A life that could have been smoother, more comfortable, more...lots of things...if I had never made the first seemingly insane step that resulted in finding out there is more to my story and to my family than I ever would have guessed.

Maybe. But that might be the essence of my story: finding out what I never knew.

There might have been less pain...less confusion...fewer sleepless night and less agonizing heart searching.

And...less life, less finding out...at a maddeningly slow pace...how much love there is...and grace...

Wow.

Chapter 3

Everybody left.
It's up to you.
Nobody cares.
They won't come through.
But tell me, God
is all this true?
Daddy, are you really
Gonna stay?
How much it hurts
Surprises me.
How wrong it seems,
How real and yet unreal,
to ask you this,
I cannot say...
JPB

Head Start: Fluoride, and Macaroni and Cheese

I began my journey through the halls of learning at age four. Three mornings a week "the blue van" came to the end of the Bliss driveway on Minthorn Lane. I clamored aboard and was whisked away to Head Start. I remember two things about Head Start. The yucky taste of fluoride and having macaroni and cheese for lunch just before being whisked back home.

When Millie Bliss took me to register for Head Start, the man at the desk had to be convinced that I was old enough to attend. I was tall for my age, but looked younger than I actually was.

"Can he write his name?"

Millie indicated that I could. They gave me a pencil and paper and I wrote it.

"Can he...can he read?"

"Give him a book."

Millie always liked to say I took the book, and "with a grin from ear to ear, read it right off."

"Well...if he can count, if he can spell, if he can write his name, he can come!"

So I attended Head Start.

After a round of activities we lay down for a bit of a break. Then they served up the mac and cheese. We sat around low round tables and devoured whatever was set before us.

Then came the worst part of the morning. We gathered in a circle and the teachers began pouring this clear, sort of funny smelling liquid into little paper cups. After we got our cups, "Do not swallow this, just swish it around in your mouth (for an incredibly long time, maybe thirty seconds), then spit it back out." So we sipped this weird smelling clear liquid that would make our teeth nice and clean. Soon after that, the van came to take us back home.

Some of us children were roaming the school halls one afternoon. There was an older boy who was bluffing, big and mean. On the bulletin board were words and he dared me to try to read them. I took one look at the board and read it. I did not really know what all the fuss was about.

I do not remember not knowing how to read. I do remember afternoons watching Sesame Street and thinking the CTW shows were not long enough. Saturday mornings, it was cartoons such as the Smurfs, and the wild Warner Brothers crowd. Wile E. Coyote and the Roadrunners was one of my favorites.

One afternoon, while watching Sesame Street, there was a singing group Do-Wopping it up. I thought it looked sort of silly...and fascinating. Grown ups in suits and ties swaying back and forth, and dancing around. It made an impression, which was buried until much later. It was my introduction to the world of jazz and rock.

Being able to read at age four did not make it easier to choke down vegetables. One day we had Brussels sprouts for lunch. My spot at the table was across from a mirror on the wall that hung between two china cupboards. I took a bite and began to choke. I looked in the mirror and the reflection of me choking made me only choke some more.

Harry Bliss made me move to a side of the table where I could not see the mirror, and I choked down the rest of my sprouts.

"I HATE Brussels sprouts!" I was forced to eat a little of it.
"There, do you like them?"

"Uh huh I (gag) like Brussels sprouts" I said, feeling queasy all over. At least the awful stuff was finally down and I could escape.

Soon it was dark, which meant it was time for bed. "Time to go to bed, all of you." (There were five of us in the house at the time, four of whom were foster children.)

"I don't WANT to go to bed!" I wailed. Since Harry was bigger and stronger than me, I went, dragging my feet and crying, to bed. And...I was sort of afraid of him.

"Do you want me to give you a spanking?"

"NOOOOOOO!"

Chapter 4

CSD Camp: This I Remember

Excitement was in the air. We were going camping up in the mountains. We were going to be a long ways away. It was going to be so much fun.

We were going to Coos Bay or somewhere. But where did not matter to a three year old. All that mattered was the excitement and the fact. We were going camping!

Never mind that it seemed to take forever to get there. Or that getting ready to go took forever. Never mind…a lot of things that never occur to a three year old.

We were going camping.

Some of the other kid's parent's were going to go too.

Would my mom be going?

Um, no, I was told. She would not be going along.

She was too drunk too often to be able to go with us to the mountains. That is what the caseworkers said.

I didn't really know what "too drunk to go up to the mountains" meant.

I did know, as much as a three or four year old could know what "mom's drunk" meant. I had seen it, although maybe I wasn't supposed to have.

I remembered…a little bit…about the afternoon I was asleep in our house. All of a sudden I woke up with a start and there she was yelling something. I didn't know what about.

I froze.

I did remember...the night time ride in the car that mom and...I was too frozen with fear, I guess, to remember who else was in the car. I did remember the sense that we were going way too fast and feeling all sorts of fear, and wondering....

Then all of a sudden the red and blue lights. And the siren. Chasing US.

Then it was over, at least for now. I did not know where every one went. I suppose it didn't matter to me at that age.

I was told, "your mom is too drunk to be able to go up with us to the mountains."

Oh, okay. She is too drunk. I didn't say anything about it to anyone...but I did think about it...a lot. I thought about that "bad fact" about my mom. Everybody knew about it. I could not tell for sure if any one really cared about it. I was too young to know if anyone would even try to do anything about it.

Any how, we were going camping. And, oh, the other fact... mom is too drunk. Well, forget her. Let's go camping.

We went camping. My mom did not come along, although she might have been able to...except she was too drunk.

That's what I was told. And it was probably true.

So we went up into the mountains and got to the camp. There was a HUGE building where we all got together and the adults made lots and lots of food.

I suppose we pigged out.

I suppose we played lots of games.

I remember only a couple things. Several of us went out in the dark to a cabin that was a distance away in the woods. I think we spent the night, although I do not remember returning to the main building the next morning.

We went swimming at the lake that was near by. There were bees or flies...bees, I think. One of the adults who were in charge went around putting stuff on our backs to keep the flies and bees away.

It must have worked, because I don't remember getting stung.

As a three or four or so year old, getting stung was a big deal. I was deathly scared of bees..and of getting hurt or doing anything bad.

Not long after CSD camp, on one of our visits, my mom brought along a guitar. Why she let her little kid loose with a guitar I will never know.

We were out in the park. I put my one foot up on a picnic table seat. And strummed away like some rock star that I wanted to be like.

I got to the end of what I was playing and leaned back. Too far back.

And lost my balance.

And fell backward. On my back with the guitar still strapped around my shoulder.

The guitar broke.

So did a lot of other things that I didn't know anything about.

The guitar...to my knowledge never got repaired or replaced.

I am not sure how many dreams blossomed and died in those few minutes.

All I knew at the time was...something really nice and special had been broken and could not be fixed.

And it was my fault...maybe.

No one ever really told me that, of course. I just...guessed. That was all I knew.

Chapter 5

Kindergarten Memories

The Blue Van.
Head Start.
The short bus.
Kindergarten.
I rode the long bus home after school.
And got whacked on the head by some high school girls in the process.

I was a brat when I was younger. An insecure, scared, frightened...and loud mouthed, yelling, laughing...brat. Well, maybe you aren't supposed to call yourself a brat. But I was.

I don't suppose the high school girls were mean, really. They probably wouldn't have paid much attention to me, except for the fact that me and my friends made a lot of noise in the bus.

We were more or less normal kids.

Normal.

I remember stuffing my face full of Halloween candy...and wearing paisleys. There are pictures of this.

I "always" had to go in for shots. And, of course, this meant I would be late for school sometimes. I did not know why I had to go get so many shots. Nobody else did...I thought.

I would hang out at Aunt Kathy's some afternoons. We cousins and whoever else was hanging around, would traipse up the road to the convenience store and get some candy. Sometimes it was ice cream.

We would be having a great time, and then Aunt Kathy would lean over toward me and whisper.

"Uh oh, look out. Here comes your mom." We all knew it was MY mom. All of us knew why Aunt Kathy said that. You never knew what my mom was going to say or do. Sometimes she could be almost nice. And other times it was terror to be within ten feet of her.

Yes, you could say we were normal kids in Pendleton, Oregon.

We were on the afternoon bus making lots of noise. Laughing about getting whacked on the head by the High School girls' drum sticks because we were being crazy and loud.

One afternoon, two of us boys were on the bus laughing and talking and being crazy as usual. One of us had a school book...I think we had finished it. We whispered something to each other and slipped to our knees and flopped the book open on the seat.

Giggling and laughing, we took a pencil and began "undressing" some of the people in a picture on one of the pages.

We drew in the pants and other things we had "taken off" and tittered that we had "taken their clothes off."

I do not remember if anyone caught on to what we were doing. Probably someone pulled our hair to make us shut up. Maybe even one of those high school girls hit us on the head with their drum sticks.

We got off the bus eventually at Minthorn Lane. The small crowd of us raced down the dirt and gravel road to our homes, glad that school was out for another day.

There was an eighth grade girl that year named Ivy who pretty much every one laughed at and made fun of. I don't even remember what she looked like. It seemed to me that Ivy was made fun of because she was weird some how. I was afraid that because everyone else knew that I was weird, that they would make fun of me. So I halfheartedly joined in the "Ivy mockery".

I have no idea if there really WAS anything the matter with Ivy. Probably there wasn't. It doesn't really matter any more, except that at that stage in life we were a bunch of kids hurting and trying hard to keep each other from hurting us and (without even knowing it) wishing that someone would hurt with us and…But, then, it was the seventies. And, well you know, the Paisleys…and Elvis, and the long hair and Viet Nam.

One afternoon, we were in class and the teacher went to the chalkboard and wrote the date, January 3, 1979. All of us kids burst out laughing.

"Teacher! It is NINETEEN EIGHTY!" We hollered. She looked at the board and put her hand to her mouth. Then she laughed…harder than we did.

So began the eighties.

<u>Chapter 6</u>

Christmas and gifts

It has always been hard for me to really enjoy Christmas. I have a few "snapshot memories" of Christmases from when I was very young.

At the Bliss's, there was one WONDERFUL Christmas. The entire day was full of fun.

The weeks before we had gone Christmas shopping and gift wrapping and everything else that goes with it. The Christmas tree was stunning...to a four or five year old.

And Christmas Eve, I even got to "turn the tree on" and make it all light up!

Gifts...lots of them. Toys...all new. Food galore. Gift wrap and ribbons and bows and boxes and fun and joy.

Christmas HAD to be the best day of the year!

The next day, I saw the "other side" of Christmas. A few of us went somewhere. I don't remember if it was one of the other kid's parent's place or just some friends. It may have even been my mom's apartment.

We did whatever we went there for, then left. We went down a long dingy hallway and past some wrapped gifts that... apparently...no one wanted or at least someone wasn't there to get them.

"Whose are those?"

"What? Oh. Someone will probably get those later. One thing sure. YOU aren't. You just got a lot of gifts for yourself."

I shuffled along. There was no use trying to explain that I had nothing of the sort in mind.

How could one day that was so fun and happy and full of joy be followed by one full of "blah"?

Forget it. Forget having any fun or enjoying anything if it is going to be snatched away like that! Although I was only four or five, I had already figured out that enjoying anything was not worth risking the possibility of having it taken away or otherwise come to an end.

Another Christmas was spent at another foster home.

I was six years old. Among other things, I was given a Cat in the Hat stuffed animal and a Peanuts collector comic book. I pretty much idolized the one and spent all the time I could poring over the other.

The following June, it became clear that I would be moving on to another home. While we were packing up my stuff, my foster mom sort of matter-of-factly said "Since you are not going to be living here and not going to be our child, we are going to keep the Cat in the Hat and the comic book."

I did not know it then, but another part of my heart died.

Years later, a mentor and I were talking. "Would you be able to forgive your foster parents for taking those things from you?"

"Why should I forgive them for taking stuff that I didn't really have any right to?"

We talked about that for a while, then:

"So you are saying you are pretty much unlovable?"

"I suppose you could say that."

A couple of days after this talk, I wrote this in my journal:

...There is an account in the life of Christ that brings up a "crazy" idea. It is during the feast of Passover. Jesus is doing one of His mind blowing things again. This time, it is washing the feet of His followers.

Peter says, in effect, "There is no way you could love me enough to be acting as my slave and washing my feet."

Jesus replies, "If you don't let me do this, you are cutting yourself off from me."

"Okay, then, make me lovable."

"What do you mean, 'make me lovable?' What's this about 'make me lovable'? Who decides who is 'lovable'?"

...What is it that revolts or stiffens at the logical conclusion of where this is going? I have been told that I am not...It has been ingrained into my subconscious center of belief that I am not...It has been "declared", perhaps "prophesied" or spoken over me that I am not...to the point that I have long agreed and accepted and lived out of the "fact" that I am not...The idea that possibly I am turns everything that I thought I had perceived and received to be true...upside down.

I guess it is that "veil being removed from the heart" thing going on.

...But what falls apart...or disintegrates...or "produces static" or interferes so that I honestly cannot "get it" or "receive it" when I hear someone...anyone...even Jesus Christ...even God Himself...say the words:

"You are lovable."

It feels like calling a bombed out shell of a building a Walmart Supercenter.

...Or a row of mounds of crumpled bricks and mortar and debris a village...or a town...or a city.

...Or a shattered pile of glass a crystal vase.

...Or desert sand a garden.

...Or a lump of clay a bar of gold.
...Or the ashes of burnt trash treasure.
...Or calling "nothing" "something".
What a frame of mind or heart to be entering Christmas...
It seems I have been here before.
I do not know what to do with this.
Another winter.
Christmas vacation.
A lot of snow.
A sudden move from Pendleton to Portland. That by all accounts caught every one by surprise. The Blisses were reportedly too old to actually follow thorough and adopt. So, I am not sure if any one really saw it coming on...
Probably someone did.
There were various trips to the Children's Services building and lots of meetings with the case workers.
There was the afternoon that one of the CSD staff had a birthday and there was cake and ice cream.
There was the toy corner where we foster kids hung out and played while the adults decided our futures.
But there was snow on the ground that last weekend in Pendleton. The Jensens came over from Portland and we spent a night at the Travelodge in town. Somewhere or how or other my stuff was packed up and loaded into their VW Rabbit.
I do not remember many of the details. I do know we went to McKay Creek School and had a look around. I had left school just before winter break, expecting to be back after break in two weeks. I had made a poster of some sort that hung on the hall wall. (This was half way through first grade.) I think I made some attempt to show them the poster and they saw the school rooms.

We probably had supper somewhere and hung out at the Travelodge. The next morning, we went out and Renae (their daughter who was a year older than I) went out and played in a snow bank in the parking lot. Then we had to hurry to the car and make the four or five hour trek to Portland...wherever that was. Over winter roads. Away from everything...I knew.

We arrived in the middle of a snow-ice storm. On the radio they were saying something about Division being closed. Whatever Division was.

I do not remember what we talked about...if we talked about anything. I was probably in too much of a turmoil of confused thoughts and feelings and questions.

Eventually we made it to Portland and Clatsop Avenue and the little two story red town house that was the Jensen's home. And I was told it was going to be my permanent home.

A few lines from a scrapbook that was compiled when I was a kid sort of sums it up.

After a long and careful search the family was found. They had indicated to another caseworker that they wanted a child to care for and love.

Joshua will miss his foster parents, Harry and Millie Bliss, as well as J, C, K, and J. They will also miss Joshua, who has been a part of their lives for a long time.

Every one knows that Joshua will be sad sometimes and that he will be upset sometimes with his new parents. But this is all right. The new parents will help Joshua understand all of these feelings, even when the feelings are not happy.

Everyone will try to help Joshua and his new parents to have a happy home with lots of caring and love. Most importantly, Joshua will have his own "Keeping parents" and home.

Chapter 7

December 1983: From Pendleton to Portland

I remember the flurry of packing. The decision was relatively sudden. The given reason was the Bliss' relatively advanced age.

My sudden leaving broke every body's hearts.

But, I did not know this. How could I have? I went through life thinking "you forgot me; I'll forget you". I had no way of knowing any different, and there was no other way to survive the trauma of yet another move.

What was real was the feeling of abrupt suddenness when I was told the Jensen's were going to take me to Portland. I can still remember the last time I went into McKay Creek School. I had a poster I had made on the wall in the hallway, and I wanted him to see it. It was during Christmas vacation, and there was a lot of snow in Pendleton.

Everything was covered with snow-and-ice in Portland.

At the Jensen's, I begged to be called by their last name. I was ashamed of my given last name, Sutter. It tied me back to the shame of having an alcoholic for a mom and really no clue about who my dad was.

Ray was a sixth grade teacher at the school. His classroom was down the hall from Primary. On the side, he was a builder. He had slightly curly hair and a full beard. His wife's name is MaryBeth. At the time they had a daughter Renae, near my age.

Just for fun, we would sometimes drink milk out of baby bottles. We would play and get crazy and then have to get a book to read and settle down.

I loved Dr. Seuss books, and could not wait for the "next one to come out".

We wore out at least one record of Horton Hears a Who! The evening How the Grinch Stole Christmas aired on TV… we watched it.

I remember the excitement of the 1984 Olympics. I would have to look it up to see where they were held. But I watched them on TV.

I also remember the three nights Superman aired on TV. It was sometime in '84, or maybe in early '85. The trilogy aired over three nights. My main memory is having to go to bed early during the first episode. I had done something I shouldn't have and this was my punishment. Later, we got videos and I got to watch the whole thing.

I remember a lot of quiet "time outs" because of how hyperactive I was.

MaryBeth told me that people laugh at what I do because it was stupid. This was on a family camping/boating trip while living with the Jensen's. They were laughing at me because what I did was stupid. I had thought they laughed because they liked the clever thing I had done.

I have a memory of being applauded during a school program (end of first year of Primary) for my part in a play by us first graders. We put it together and performed it (of course, with the help of the teachers). I could not bring myself to accept or enjoy the applause. It was a very first-grade-level thing about four snowmen getting melted in the sun.

Some of us in the class played various instruments. At first I wanted to play the xylophone. I played with the idea of the bass drum. I loved its soft mallets that made such a sweet booming sound. I later asked (I think) to be moved to the acting part, for reasons I cannot recall or explain.

My act seemed to have gone better...so the teachers said... (meaning, I put more into the acting than my fellow actors) than the others. I could not accept that I was able to be good on the stage. The next day they were going to watch a video of it. For some reason the machine did not work. I was glad to not have to be embarrassed with watching my own performance.

I think that even back then I had a sense of not being good enough for anything. I do not remember being really accepted among my classmates at school. I do not know if I thought I did not deserve success and applause, or could not bring myself to believe that I was actually good enough to be applauded. I am not really sure I know if I thought I mattered. I do not know what I wanted.

Close to the end of the school year, Catlin Gabel has what they call Primary Overnights (an annual Friday evening-Saturday morning camp-out at school). I suppose they still have these. Primary was set up so that you took it twice. So in a way, I went to first grade twice, in two different schools. I was sent with a message for some sixth graders. I must have stuttered it out or something; but they did not pay any attention to it.

I don't remember much about the Overnights, except that my night began in the tent...but I woke up inside the school building. I do remember seeing and being impressed that Sandy (one of the teachers) was in a sleeping bag on the grass under the stars.

I remember at 6 ½ inexplicably peeing my pants at school. It was almost last period, and I was told to go to "the quiet area" we could take books to read" and lay low and dry out and wait for school to be over. This sort of reconfirmed that I was dumb and stupid. I do not even remember what the outcome was once I got home.

I had a reputation as a crazy loudmouth, or "a maniac".

I "sucked" in gym, so much so that the gym teacher listed me as a year younger than I actually was in order to give anything close to a passable grade.

My physical and muscular development was so poor that something had to be done about it. Every afternoon, I walked three or four times around the block. I got my exercise, rain or shine. Rain coat or shorts and tees...I was out there. I guess I became a familiar sight.

I suppose my muscle tone got a little better through it all.

We had to write stories; and draw pictures to go with them. I eventually found out that mine were considered too far fetched to make sense of.

Somewhere around this time, during Experiential Days, I almost drowned at a farm and developed an almost hysterical fear of water.

The next school year, I did something related to architecture for Experiential Days.

There was a woodworking shop class at Catlin Gabel. I made a simple wood telephone.

I had vague interest in woodworking as a first grader, which was never really encouraged.

I took Brownie (my worn out but still clung to teddy bear that I had since age two) along with me to the Jensen's in Portland. I was a hyperactive, possibly retarded, emotionally disturbed boy that they did not need on their hands. Suddenly, one day, I was told I was going to go out to Estacada (wherever that was, somewhere about thirty minutes out of Portland). There was a Mennonite family that was going to take me in.

The Jensen family was going to adopt me, so why didn't they? Because of a number of things. I had been pulled out of a previous home (I thought THAT was going to be "for good") and put into a totally new situation. I proved to be an emotional mess. Among the complaints were laughing at wildly inappropriate times, apparent lack of common sense. This led to the conclusion that I was not "all there"...pretty much a helpless case. (They even took me to get checked by a psychologist. I was diagnosed as being in really bad emotional, mental shape.) Any plans to adopt me came to a swift, sudden end. I have since seen copies of the evaluations. According to them, I was, in fact, a nervous and emotional mess. Not far from needing to be institutionalized.

Also, about that time, a near relative of the Jensen's had committed suicide. This relative had had some mental issues. So there was more than just one reason that they were unable to keep me.

When it became clear that I was not going to stay at the Jensen's, I slipped into a subdued form of survival mode.

I was about six years old, a very hyperactive "brat". I did not know how to relate to people my age or older. I was a nuisance among my classmates, made too much noise in general and was more or less a class misfit.

My hand eye coordination is not the best. The time it takes me to verbalize thoughts is longer sometimes than for the normal person. The cooperation between my eyes and inside my brain is quite far from good. These are a few of the effects of being exposed to alcohol and marijuana before birth.

So, once again I was going to be sent somewhere else.

Maybe this time "it" would work out.

So, things began taking shape that led to the hills of Estacada.

"What on earth is so funny?"

"I don't know. Nothing."

"Will you STOP laughing and look at me when I am trying to talk to you?"

I plunged into helpless tittering and outright giggling. I tried to stop, honestly. I tried to "just listen". But I simply could not.

"WHAT is so funny?"

"I don't know...um..."

I fell into more helpless giggles.

"The wrinkles in your forehead when you scowl like that...I dunno..."

"I don't know." That was my stock answer to lots of questions. There is a fancy word called *confabulate* that describes what I did quite well. That, or it was a way of "turning off my mind". Which was something I did pretty often.

That was me at the age of six. I was...hyperactive. Out of control. LOUD. Laughing at...nothing. The next minute, depending on what was said to me, I could be crying and shedding torrents of tears. Crying...about nothing.

I was told that I should have been put on Ritalin. I was supposed to be sent to the public school in Estacada. I am not sure why I wasn't. In a way it was a good thing that I wasn't.

It was actually extreme. If someone said "but" my mind instantly went south, and I would laugh almost mindlessly. Minutes later, I would be SO ashamed of how I laughed about...nothing. I would get really mad at myself. Confused. Why was I like this? Not just sometimes. A lot of the time.

I remember being really afraid...of what? I am not sure, exactly. That MaryBeth was always angry at me? That Renae (their daughter who was about a year older than me) was always telling on me for all the stupid things I did?

We both loved Dr. Seuss Books. And Madeline books. And Babar the Elephant and the "Shape People" books. We both had a "special shelf" where we kept our favorite things safe.

I thought Renae was almost perfect. At least, she was not always walking straight into door jams and getting huge "eggs" on her forehead. I was the one who was always yelling at school and at the same time always stumbling into stuff like the steps on the slides. I was the one who got labeled a "maniac" by the big guys. And for embarrassingly good reasons. I was the one who peed himself during school and had to hang out in the reading area until I dried out and it was time to go home.

I do not remember the trip to Dr. Boverman. Or the one to Dr. Schimschock. I do remember having to go to doctors lots and hating that this was one other proof that I was different from the other kids. I have read the records of some of those visits to those doctors, and the general thought was that I was mildly to severely retarded.

This was the main reason, or at least, it was one of the given reasons, that plans to adopt me fell through. Later, I learned that someone in the family had committed suicide and that played a part in the decision.

And, I suppose, that was enough of a reason.

So first there were visits by Silvia, the caseworker. This was starting to be "old hat". My life had been controlled by caseworkers. I soon began catching on that I wasn't going to be at Jensen's "forever" after all.

One day Silvia took me to a park in Portland. She asked me "What kind of a house would you like to live in?" There was a high rise apartment building within sight of the park bench we were sitting on. "I wanna live in an apartment building like that over there." We both laughed and knew that was not really the kind of house I wanted to live in.

Silvia broke it to me slowly that it was not working out at Jensen's, and that they were looking for another family to take me in. My heart sank. Again. Why? Who were these people? Would they even really want me? Silvia said the family was Mennonite, whatever that was. They were people who didn't believe in doing certain things, I was told. Like you couldn't wear shorts. I was told they probably wouldn't let you have the Cat in the Hat stuffed animal, or the Peanuts comic book I had been given for Christmas.

The Jensen's kept those. I did keep the rest of the stuffed animals, and I was able to keep Sam I Am. Why I would be able to have Sam I Am and not the Cat in the Hat was beyond me. But then, pretty much everything was beyond me.

I had books...lots of them.

In the course of several rides in the car with Silvia, I found out more about the Bechtel family. They lived in the country not too far from a little town called Estacada. Silvia asked me what I thought and how I felt about this change...again. I struggled to know, and it was hard to say what I was thinking about all of this. It had happened so many times before. Did it have to happen again? Would these people decide they wouldn't want me, too, after a while?

As a six year old, I came up with a lot of conclusions on my own. I began to believe that the more you can keep your confusion and pain inside, the better everything will be.

I think it was a Thursday or Friday afternoon when we made the long drive out to Estacada. I asked repeatedly how many miles it was. I took a pen and paper and drew a "map" of the very curvy road out to Estacada. We finally got there.

The plan was that I would spend the night, and maybe be there for the weekend. That soon changed when Silvia found out that they were going to some camp or meetings or something. So I was there only one night.

I think the youth group came over for the evening, and they played volleyball in the front yard. For me, someone introduced me to the Bible. I was fascinated that there was a book called Joshua. I do not remember much about the rest of that evening. I think I went out and "helped" with chores.

I was nervous. Scared. Should I hope? I did want to be "good enough" that these people would keep me. But could I be good enough? After all, I hadn't been good enough for the people I had lived with the last year and a half.

Chapter 8

First Impressions of...The Mennonites.

People who…Do not believe in wearing shorts. Do not have TV. (Why not? I had no clue…and it probably wouldn't have made much difference if I did know.) Probably wouldn't let you listen to Magic 107, which I loved to listen to. For over a year, my alarm clock woke me up with this station every morning.

The Mennonites...some of them don't let you wear flip flops...the "worldly ones" do. I discovered this to my seven year old shock one afternoon when several families went thrift store shopping. I am amazed at how quickly I clung to this new...whatever it was...identity. "They said" so it must be true. For instance...

"We don't believe in TV."

"We don't believe in Santa."

I had no idea what all this was about. I did know that I had gone from home to home to this home and...would I maybe get it right this time?

As far as I could tell, I had no identity. I was the "brat" that the older kids at Catlin Gabel called a "maniac". My mom was "a drunk", and it almost did not occur to me to wonder about my dad.

Sometime in the previous year, while living with the Jensens, we had gone to the zoo and OMSI. As we were going around the exhibits and doing all the things a kid would do, I noticed a group of people dressed "kind of funny." (They were actually dressed in conservative Mennonite attire, which I would be accustomed to later.)

I forgot about this incident, until years later.

I stayed at the Bechtel's one night and left some time the following morning. I do not remember much more about that morning, except one thing that I never told any one.

I wet the bed.

In light of the confusion and the whirlwind of uncertainty, it probably is no surprise.

I did not tell any one.

I was scared.

Silvia took me back to the Jensen's, where…we wore shorts. My belongings were soon going to be gathered up and loaded into Silvia's car. All my books. The cage I had made out of a square of plywood and four two by twos uprights wrapped around with chicken wire. It came along, full of clothes or books.

The telephone I made in shop that was yellow and green… came along.

There were some things that did not come along, that were mine. At least, I had been told at the time that they were mine. Like the journals with the wildly imaginative story lines that I wove. And The Cat in the Hat stuffed animal that I totally adored.

This might be part of why I buried any interest in writing for a long time. Or any interest in anything beside trying to survive. At least, outwardly I appeared to be surviving.

The next to last day at the Jensen's I walked around the block like I had done for most of the previous year...rain or shine. And I told people in the area bye.

The next morning, Silvia arrived and we loaded my stuff in her car and we drove up Clatsop and out toward Estacada and life among these people called Mennonites.

I am almost sure I did not cry when I left Jensens. I do remember feeling sort of sad....confused...lost...wondering about a lot of things that a kid who is only six years old is not supposed to wonder about.

When it seems that no one really "gets" you...what are you supposed to do? I stuffed it, or at least, made a violent attempt at stuffing it. Of course it stuck out all over and was an undeniable mess, in spite of all of my efforts. I convinced myself that you are not supposed to cry or show emotion, and made a mess in the course of trying not to do it.

So I felt like an identity was snatched away. And another one flung in front of me. So I lunged and grabbed it...what ever it was...for dear life. I came to hate anything related to adoption...hated when any one mentioned that I was a foster child, and later, adopted.

Hated is not too strong of a word. I was ashamed of the facts of my life. I thought I was the blame for a lot of things. I thought that I was bad, and two or three foster homes that wouldn't or couldn't keep me proved it. For several years, I was almost sure that I would "have to" move on to another family.

I remember sitting on the bed after the flurry of unpacking and getting settled in...and just thinking. And wondering.

Somewhere along the line, mom took me along to the house of "someone who sold Bibles." We drove about four miles up into the foothills and after curves and trees and hills (some of them steep, and curvy) we got to the Bontrager's.

In the window near the front door was a small sign that had probably been there for years. "Prevent TRUTH decay. Read the Bible."

An old man came to the door and welcomed us in and he helped us select a Bible that was "just right for me."

I kept that Bible for a long time. In fact, I still have it. It is little, small and worn, but carries many memories with it.

Mom told me Ernest was the Bishop of the church. I had no idea what a bishop is…I looked up and up at him and marveled at his deep low voice. And his kind smile. Eventually I would find out that he told the best stories. And his sermons were the most interesting combination of Bible study and one story after another.

I remember a few things about my first Sunday at Porter Mennonite Church. My Sunday School class was in the "little room" up by the amen corner. Just past the door that was almost never opened, except when the auditorium got too hot in the summertime.

We read out of little booklets called quarterlies. The lesson was from something called one of the prophets. I remember reading out loud about someone who was a "son of Idiot"… and was told the name was actually "Iddo". Whatever.

Then the "after service." I did not know what that meant. I kind of still don't…but that is what it was called.

I do not remember the sermon. I was not used to Mennonite services. I do remember Ernest preached. And I suppose my mind wandered. We were sitting in a plain almost drab room. There were windows on both sides. Behind the pulpit, or "sacred desk" was a bench for the other ministers. I found out later there was a pull out black board that sometimes did not easily come out when the speaker needed it. The track it was on in the wall froze up or rusted in the fall and winter.

Ernest ended the sermon and sat down.

They sang a song. I say that, because I sat there and stared at Ernest. For some reason, he did not sing. (It wasn't until later that I learned that he sang a beautiful strong bass and (I heard) could switch to tenor whenever he wanted to.) I was certain that he was going to die on the spot. That is why I stared and stared.

He didn't die. And I grew up eventually to have a lot of respect for him.

Chapter 9

Trying to learn to color
Means I'm not staying in the lines...
The colors getting smudged together
Look a mess sometimes.
You wave your perfect picture
In my face...to inspire me, I guess...
The only thing it tells me
Is my paper looks a mess.
I know I've broken crayons
And the sight may you appall...
But just because I messed it up...
Do you have to break them all?
You have your name on pictures...
I'm doing good to hold a pen...
Is it too much to ask you
To remember where you've been?
I know it looks pathetic
And my smudges will never do...
But give me time, there's a chance that I
May color as good as you.
JPB

There are some things I hesitate to write about because I am afraid of how it will be taken. I do not want to sound like everything about my childhood was bad...because there were parts of it that were good. And the alternative would have been worse than what my life actually was. That does not mean I have very many good feelings about how my life was growing up.

I do not even know if it is okay to admit that. I do not even know if it is okay to admit that there are a lot of things that I am still confused, and sad, and angry about. Did I say angry? I meant mad...enraged...infuriated, to tell the exact, and far from pretty truth. I have been told there are a lot of beautiful things about me. I haven't been able to see very many of them. I suppose this means that I do not believe.

Believe...what does that beautiful sounding word mean, anyway?

If I believe in a loving merciful God, does that mean I will deny the pain of life? I don't know, although I have been told the answer is yes. But how can it? A girl with leukemia goes into the hospital for surgery. Does her trust in the goodness and skill of the surgeons erase the pain? Yes, I know...she is "put to sleep" during the surgery. But afterward...There is undeniably pain afterward. Because there is life.

A boy loses a limb and somehow experiences phantom pains. These are supposed to be very real. And I have no doubt that they are.

So there are pains caused by what we experienced and pains caused by what we were deprived of. Is it ever wise or good to deny the fact of either?

If "honor" as used in the Bible means to recognize the weight of someone's influence in your life...recognizing some things...pleasant or otherwise...needs to be done sometimes.

Such as...honor your father. I honestly do not know how to do that without sounding hateful or spiteful or vengeful or mean. Or as far as it goes...feeling those things.

It is hard for me to believe...there is that word again...in the goodness and Fatherhood of God. I have to admit that I find it very hard to connect "father" with "goodness". It is easy to connect "father" with "control or a lot of other words.

There are a lot of things I do not understand about my relationship with my adoptive dad. Those two words bring things to mind that I do not even want to bring up. I am not sure why I am bringing them up.

Mostly because I am trying to retrace my steps through life and find God.

And find why He seems so...hard to find...or please...or know.

Part of the "honoring"...owning...healing...maybe?

I hope so. It would be hard to come up with a reason otherwise.

It is hard to come up with a reason for doing this, the way it is.

I do not know why, really, but Saturdays were often nerve wracking for me. It was not because we had pancakes on

Saturday. It wasn't even because we often went to Salem to Grandpa and Grandma Brothers.

One Saturday dad was angry at me because I was eating my pancakes too fast. After the others were excused, dad came over to where I was sitting and crammed my mouth full of pancakes.

"Now, chew."

I did.

I don't know if that is why, but Saturday breakfast was nearly always traumatic after that. My stomach would literally knot up with tension. (Dad tolerated little or no laughing or talking at table.) It got to the point that peanut butter would "land like a rock" in my stomach and it was all I could do to prevent choking it back up.

Thus Saturday would begin. Sometimes it would go from bad to worse and sometimes it would stay the same. Sometimes I was under so much tension that my internals would feel like a solid mass.

Then Sunday we would go to church.

Where I would be able to relax. Somewhat. But not totally. How could I really when I was required to paste a smile over a confused...shattered...angry...lost...inside?

So I would sit in church and hope against hope that my insides would not "grumble". But they usually did, and rumbled so loud that I was sure every one could hear it.

I cannot explain why I would almost helplessly laugh during church, during the sermon, of all times. Dad would nudge me and motion me to be quiet. The more I tried to be quiet the worse it got. I became so wildly ashamed of myself that I could not bear to look any one in the eye.

At the same instant that I would be laughing uncontrollably I would be inwardly screaming why am I laughing when really there is nothing funny??! I hate this..I hate myself.

At home, I would swing from convulsive crying to hysterically laughing, with no rhyme or reason to any of it.

There was one shameful Sunday morning that I laughed so uncontrollably during the sermon, that dad ordered me to go out to the back.

I froze. I desperately tried to stop. I can't. I can't keep on laughing like this. I can't stand the shame of parading out to the back.

I disobeyed that time and did not go out.

I cannot say how ashamed and mortified and full of self hatred I was. I couldn't understand myself at all.

I knew it was all my fault...that there was something wrong with me somehow. I just knew I was strange...different... inferior to my friends.

Friends? I was not even sure I really had any.

And I did not know that my mind would be stretched, my endurance would be challenged, or that my heart would be cracked open and almost shattered a number of times in those next months.

Chapter 10

If you were there...
Why couldn't I sense you?
If you really cared
Why didn't you come through?
Why did it seem
You let it fall to pieces
If you were there...
Why didn't you come through?
I'm sure that I
Have no right to question.
But human need
Sometimes trumps what is right.
I'm caught between
Trying to say the "right thing"
And believing
'Though none of it seems right.
You laid down laws
Seemed to say "don't question"
Maybe you had
Another thing in mind...?
Maybe you hoped
Our love of the forbidden
Would drive us to

Seek the love you had to hide.
So you allowed
My life to give wrong answers
Perhaps I got
Your thoughts toward me all wrong.
Perhaps the words
I thought were condemnation
Were how you chose
To draw me to you song!
JPB

"Confessions of a self abusing kid"

I am not sure when it began.

It was a mixture of subconscious self hatred...and hatred of my mom.

Perhaps a silent death wish that began...I don't really remember when.

There was a book in Primary at Catlin Gabel about a girl that was captured by aliens and taken apart and turned into a robot.

I would read that book over and over...always drawn in to the strangely horrifying, yet intriguing, yet almost exciting story of someone being totally taken apart and put back together.

Something about being absolutely helpless in the hands of your destroyer, who was somehow now, suddenly able to control you and make you into something horrid...of his choosing.

Was this my first image of what God might be like?

And, in a sickly, helpless almost guilty way, I kind of liked the feeling that came with reading books like that.

Why not enjoy stories about people's lives being destroyed? Mine was destroyed from the word go...so I thought. And that was true, partly.

The being destroyed part was the side I could see...and that made sense.

I could not imagine anyone trying to do me any "good"....

Or that my "real family" might actually miss me...

Because it was obvious to me that they didn't. No one cared...probably.

Then I moved to Estacada...and lived among the Mennonites.

And they had a book, an old book...about innocent people being brutally murdered for no reason. Except that they did not have the right religion.

And they were called a word that I thought vaguely might mean the same as "hero".

The book was *Martyr's Mirror*.

The text of this huge book is somewhat boring, the entire book is somewhat morose. The main reason this book was published in the 1700's was to remind American Mennonites what their ancestors had endured back in Europe.

And there were frankly graphic pictures in this book.

Pictures of...death. People getting tortured. Helpless people at the mercy of people who had monstrous amounts of power over...people who were wrong enough...foolish enough to disagree with or stand up to their tyranny.

What would it be like to be...crucified? How would it feel to be chained (maybe naked) to a stake and burned to death? What would it be like to be terribly tortured and murdered?

The idea of being shamed was not a new thing to me. I breathed shame. As far as I knew, I was a shame.

It would probably serve me right to be absolutely shamed like that. I could just picture it. Stripped to the skin, probably tortured...hung up by my heels or something, brutally flogged... and maybe my life would be destroyed in the most degrading, humiliating, painful, terrible way possible. Because that was all I could imagine that I deserved.

I could not imagine anyone coming through for me at the last minute. Why should anyone? Did anyone even care that I existed...let alone give a damn about what that existence was like?

So, I imagined terrible, shameful, degrading death scenes, with me as the "victim"...and no help, or rescue, or mercy... nothing. A vile life destroyed, because it deserved to be destroyed.

Of course, I knew I would not be allowed to say "I want to kill myself" out loud. I knew this, because "suicide is a one way ticket to hell...and you don't want to go to hell."

Somewhere down inside, I snorted, *I am already in a hell. Who would care?*

Out loud, I just shrugged and stared off blankly into space.

I don't know if mom and dad would have allowed me to read *Martyr's Mirror* or *Fox's Book of Martyrs* if they would have had any idea I was more or less getting a sadistic arousal every time I read the books, or saw any of the pictures.

It had more or less the same effect as porn.

Except it included a perverted twist.

I began fantasizing...dreaming...and acting out. I would dream about killing, and being killed, by turns.

I would fantasize about being torturer, and executioner, and then I would be the tortured and murdered...and sometimes in beyond bizarre manner.

I harbored a secret fetish, that I knew I would never be allowed to admit out loud.

This is not to say *Martyr's Mirror* or *Fox's Book of Martyrs* or any related books are wrong.

It is to say that I had a self hatred, near death wish that, when confronted with stories and pictures of this kind, opened a door to an agreement with Satan.

I dwelt on death, in the name of being interested in history...facts...Christian history, in fact.

I was drawn to any account that had someone being severely, brutally tortured and murdered because of what they believed.

Then one afternoon I was introduced to what is called soft porn, on the way home from school.

I pretended to not be really interested. Of course, there was no point in trying to act as if I thought I would be able to sneak it into the house.

But that did not stop me from snatching glances in catalogues...and a few attempts at cross dressing.

Of course, this was when no one was around.

I have no idea what dad would have done if he would have found out any of this. I do know what he did one afternoon when he found a small cardboard with the "f word" cut out on it.

He more or less did...nothing.

As far as I knew, "the f word" was the worst word you could say...and since it was so bad (I thought) and since it was used so often as a vulgar, and usually degrading curse word...I often used it...to curse myself.

And since I was obviously so bad...and unwanted, and worthless, it made total sense to curse myself with every terrible name and word that could possibly come to mind, and there were lots of them.

The day came that mere fantasizing was not enough. I began to act out, when I was certain no one would be able to see...and at some of the most bizarre times, and in the strangest places.

Why?

If you would have asked me, I would have muttered, "Why not? I am shit, so I may as well treat myself like it. No one else is treating me as terribly as I deserve...and I deserve to be treated like shit, so why not?"

I would go out to the barn at chore time, sometimes in the dead of winter, and strip myself to the skin, in a room in the back that I was almost certain no one would catch me by surprise. I was compelled to make myself feel a tiny bit of what I was sure I deserved.

One evening I got a really bizarre idea. I gathered a number of somewhat large rags that reminded me of what I imagined slave clothes or what prisoners would have on in Roman times, and that night, I went to bed wearing these rags.

I did this for several nights.

Then one afternoon, mom came into my room and spotted the rags I had stashed behind the bed.

"What are you doing with all these rags?"

I muttered a lie about using them when I dusted and forgetting to put them away.

I forget what mom said, but she gathered the rags, saying something about she wondered where all the rags had gotten to, and then left my room.

How could you...logically...tell me I was doing wrong? It did feel a bit weird. But I was allowing my imagination to try to play out what it might have been like.

It is strange to dream of...to fantasize...to have a near death wish of being brutally, violently mutilated and destroyed... if not at your own hand, then at the hand of someone else...

unless you are so sure you are undeserving of life that death is too good for yourself.

And that is pretty much where I was at one point.

Why shouldn't I? Wasn't I the kid that apparently no foster home could really keep? And hadn't I heard mom herself admit that adopting us was probably a mistake?

And didn't I know...too much?

Around this time I also began abusing myself physically. I would fly into a towering rage at something I had done, and rail at myself, calling down unprintable names, and then, because that was not enough, I would hit myself across the side of the face. Hard. Repeatedly. Usually when no one was around.

Why should any one see? What would they do, pretend to care?

I did this often enough, was driven into fits of rage often enough that I became a nervous wreck.

I would get severe headaches. My eyes would throb, and I smacked myself across the side of the face often enough that I may have caused some blood vessel weakening or damage.

But did I care? Not really. For all I knew, I deserved any level of pain I got, mostly for the terrible crime of simply existing.

Meanwhile, my vocal cords began showing the effects of the nervous, angry strain I placed then under from all the teeth gritting and fighting valiantly to keep it all in or at least under cover.

It eventually affected my already halting speech.

I would be sitting in sunday school and we would be reading around the room. My turn would come, way too soon, and I would feel a catch, almost choking sensation in my throat when I would try to read.

It just added to the embarrassed shame I already felt.

Added to the frustration of not being able to talk as well as my sibling, hence, not as good as I should have been able to if I were normal, was the fact that I was informed constantly that I simply did not want to sing.

In the Mennonite circles, being able to sing sort of determines your status: where you are on the totem pole.

If you can sing, there are doors open to you on all sides. Especially if you are a guy who can sing well, have a good voice and are able to carry both yourself and a tune in public, you are going places. This, added to the ability to speak well in public, put you on the eventual track toward getting ordained one day.

None of those applied to me. So I never really "went anywhere".

Of course, I would be asked to have topics after I joined church. And to be honest, I almost begged for commendation after the services. Mostly to brace myself for the scathing, devastating criticism and cut down of every public speaking attempt I would have in church, after we got home.

So...what was I supposed to believe: those who told me that my efforts at public speaking were coming along, or those whose who almost destroyed my will, want or desire to talk in public: my parents?

I believed my parents. And believed that my public speaking was abominable, always going to be attacked for doing the wrong thing, a mysterious thing called "acting like someone you aren't" not looking at the audience (how could I bear to, especially given that I eventually came to guess that everyone shared my parent's opinion of how crappy my public speaking was?)

I actually refused to consider that my eyesight might have something to do with that. I was just a dumb kid who was almost too awkward to be allowed to try to talk in public. But in the Mennonite church, when you are asked to have a topic, you are pretty much expected to say yes. To refuse might be an indication that you are not "doing very well spiritually".

Most of the time I was not doing "very well spiritually".... but since appearances must be maintained...I did my share of topics. The last thing I wanted was for the preachers to come and talk to me. Not just about what was "wrong" spiritually....I quickly came to the conclusion that not only did I not want to get in trouble with them, I was not good enough to even think about talking to them...about anything.

So I could not keep from abusing myself. I wanted... needed...pain. Shame. I deserved to have everyone angry at me.

I was a walking time bomb...never knowing when I was going to get provoked into flying off the handle. I figured out that I was good for very little.

The only thing I could think of that I was even close to good enough for was working...and I instinctively knew I barely did an acceptable job at that.

I lived under a cloud of "why can't you be like the others in this family? Why do you have to be so different from everyone else in school? Or church?"

Why was I the only one in my circle of friends who did not seem to be athletic enough to even swing a bat and hit a softball? Or have such a poor swing that it was pointless to play outfield. Once in a while (even to my own shock) I was able to catch fly balls in a game. Rarely was I able to make a hit that amounted to anything.

And it would have been pointless for me to even try to pitch. I did good to get the ball within the general vicinity of the player I was throwing toward. If I would have tried to pitch, I would have given the other team many, many walks.

I joined in games of this nature because it was required... not because I wanted to or was very able to.

I know all about being chosen last for pretty much any game.

I dreaded being chosen to be "it".

You could not have convinced me that I was good...at anything.

Because everything I knew said that I was stupid.

What else caused me to have such embarrassingly halting speech? What other reason was there for never being able to say even close to what was on my mind? What difference would it have made if I would have felt free to explore and find out what I was really interested in, as a youngster?

I had what was passed off as a passing whim to get a keyboard and learn to play it...as silly as that sounds now. I was told I would lose interest in a couple of weeks, so that never happened.

I flirted briefly with the idea of learning how to draw, but since I could never "get it" good enough in my own eyes, I eventually buried any inclination toward drawing.

I lived under enough tension at home that I was pretty much afraid to talk. Why bother? I would be called down or laughed at or made to feel stupid, or just ignored if I tried to say anything.

So I would be quiet at the table and just eat...and then get criticized for eating too fast.

It made perfect sense to me: no one was interested in what I thought or had to say...when I did open my mouth what came out sounded garbled and I was sure it made no sense...especially to the rest of the family who always made sense when they talked, and always had the right words.

Why shouldn't I have hated myself?

Why shouldn't have I smacked myself silly in total frustration and anger?

I was literally powerless to control my anger, my frustration, my self abuse. I was careful to not let it show around certain people...just because you are supposed to save face. Or something.

I professed to be a Christian...at least I was a church member through all of this. A powerless church member with so little evidence of being born again it shocks me now to recall how I was told, over and over, that I was.

So one day in total desperation I prayed "Jesus, I am tired of getting angry all the time. Please help me to get over my anger."

The next day was positively terrible.

I read my Bible, and prayed, as I did pretty much every morning, and as we were instructed was almost the only way to have victory during the day, after becoming a Christian.

Then I stepped out of my bedroom and my day flew apart.

It felt as if I sinned in the very act of getting up...and stepping out of the room...I did my morning chores and by appearances my very actions turned against me as I did them.

It was impossible to please anyone, all day long.

The more I tried to do what I was supposed to, the worse it got.

By supper, I was beyond livid. I was uncontrollably angry, at myself...because I could do nothing good enough to keep people from getting angry at me, and that was more than reason (in my mind) to be beyond angry and physically abusive of myself.

Everyone else seemed to think they had to do this nice, nice sweet talk and try to assure me it would be ok (I knew it could never be ok) and that they forgave me (I knew there was nothing about me that came close to worthy of being forgiving.)

Why would anyone be stupid enough to forgive someone who was...a sin? Not, someone who committed sin, as in "did wrong"...but was a sin...

Because I was convinced that that is exactly what I was...a sin...my parent's sin.

It took me years to undo the web of that belief.

I could see no way around the idea that I was my parent's sin. Therefore, because you forgive people for doing, not "being" sin...since I was a sin...there was no way I could be forgiven, to say nothing of born again or saved.

I convinced myself I was my parent's mistake, and that this is why everything happened in my life the way it did.

So there was no reason to ask God to forgive me, since I was a sin. And there was no reason to forgive anyone for anything that happened to me, because it was all my fault. I deserved all the bad that came my way.

Didn't I?

I was angry at myself for being a sin. I was angry at my parents for what I was sure was purposeful abandonment. I was angry at myself for existing. I was angry at God...for not stopping it. For allowing...or causing it or...I was in too much of a turmoil of heart and mind to even know if I was thinking logically.

I would go for a few days, or maybe a week on a somewhat even keel, and everything seemed to be fine. Then, something would come up and trigger my temper and I would fly off the handle.

I would cuss myself out...using words that probably made the devils blush. And more or less wish, or speak, or scream, or hiss myself to hell.

I could not think. I could not control my thoughts, or my voice. I was probably mildly possessed...or at least heavily oppressed...by the devil himself.

So...what reason did I have to even think about forgiving anyone? In my mind, no one had really "wronged me." I deserved everything I got, that was bad...didn't I? I was "the wrong"...I was the "thing" that was probably unforgivable. I was the "piece of shit" that was not really supposed to be here (but horrible fact...I was) and was in everyone's way and more or less tolerated.

But no one was honest enough to say to my face that I was in the way (a few came close to it). No one really told me I was hated...in so many words. And no one suggested that I be "gotten out of the way." No one even suggested that I punish myself.

I came up with that idea on my own. I began imagining ways to get rid of myself...ways that I was too scared to even try. Because I knew (I was taught quite well) that taking your own life was an unforgivable, one way ticket to the flames of hell.

So? Life was basically hell. It was hard to imagine why I should not go to where I deserved to go sooner than later, since I so obviously belonged there and for all I knew originated there.

I imagined bizarre things...like building a scaffold with a fire under it (I was going to hell anyway, what was the difference?), and throwing a rope around my neck and tying it off around my neck and waiting for the fire under the scaffold to burn through and...there I would be...hanged and (probably) burning to death.

Why not? I could not think of a single reason not to except that I was scared.

And...instinctively I knew it would make mom and dad look and feel terrible. Part of me wanted to and part of me didn't.

For sure, I knew no one would understand. For crying out loud, no one really understood me the way it was.

I had one overarching thought about myself: I am unwanted because I am bad, or stupid, or both. Everything I could see pointed to this "truth".

Why not? I was in a foster home where I was the youngest of eight. And they were smart. I wasn't. They had their lives "together"...I didn't. They talked...and talked "well"...and I couldn't...and everyone took it on them to either ignore what this stupid kid was trying to say, or finish his stupidly halting sentences.

And it seemed everyone made sure I knew they thought I was different...or stupid...or retarded.

Of course, I was retarded...normal people do not stutter or lose their train of thought mid sentence.

Dad even said I was mildly retarded or something.

Of course it was true.

Wasn't it?

So...I would become violently angry at myself. I would be in my room, seething, cursing myself...and that was not quite enough. I knew I deserved worse treatment.

I smacked myself as hard as I could across the side of my face. Sometimes three times in a row (one time I did it five times). Why shouldn't I have?

What would have been the point of telling anyone? Oh yes, I would have been severely condemned for being self abusive. Why ask for that, I was condemned inwardly the way it was, and did not need any outside confirmation of what was boiling inside.

This may not have been the actual cause of the extreme headaches I began to get during school.

I began to complain about getting severe eye and headaches in sixth grade or so. Sometimes I actually felt as if my head was hollow.

It did not seem that anyone believed me.

We went to a children's hospital in Portland, and in the course of a battery of tests, it was found out that "you have 20/20 vision...get out of here"...more or less.

The headaches, that mom and dad probably believed I fabricated (they thought I fabricated everything else....it seemed) continued...and persisted.

So I was told to take niacin for the headaches. And later, something called bilberry.

Nothing helped.

I was obviously faking the headaches (except they were literally killing me).

I survived school, somehow, punctuated with headaches that I was told I was faking.

At the same time, the only half way safe place in my life was school (this was in high school)...and I found out that I was in trouble for latching or clinging to my high school teacher.

I felt hated at home and this teacher at least acted as if he was half way interested in me as a person.

And I was...taking too much of his time.

So I was crushed. I was hated at home, and too much for my teacher at school.

As far as I could tell, I was too much...and yet not enough...for anyone...or anything.

I still had no idea how come I had these severe headaches...mom and dad more or less thought I was making it up. I was almost dying.

I was close to suicidal.

I was totally unprepared for what was coming next.

Chapter 11

Remember what they used to say
When you were three or four?
You asked a lot of questions
And asked and asked some more...
Then the answer you would get
That sounded real grand:
"Just wait till you get older,
And then you'll understand."
And we say,
Well, I got older...
But I still don't understand.
This life throws lots of questions
That there are no answers to...
And even spoken answers
Sometimes do not ring true.
They say when we're in heaven
We'll see the larger plan...
Tho I know we'll stand in wonder
I'm not so sure we'll understand.
'Cause we'll say
Well, I got older...
But I still don't understand.
Maybe we'll gradually be shown

What it was all about.
Maybe the seeds of wonder
Are sown in times of doubt.
Maybe the answer—when it comes—
Will not be all that plain.
If we eternally "get older"...
He may more and more explain.
Still we'll say...
Well, I got older,
But I still don't understand.
JPB

Up in White Smoke

Expressing myself on paper has always been easier than with spoken words. I do not remember when I realized I liked reading and writing poetry. I loved anything by Shel Silverstein. I devoured any Dr. Seuss book I could find. I loved books such as Babar the Elephant and devoured the Madeline books.

I loved to read almost as long as I can remember. I actually could read before first grade. All of us in the first grade I attended were reading in first grade. I did not know until later, that "most people learned to read in first grade".

It was no big deal. I had gone through Head Start and Kindergarten and two years of first grade in two schools before second grade. And I had written some "wildly imaginative stories" in Primary at Catlin Gabel in Portland.

Drawing interested me a little when I was in school. But none of this really explains why I enjoy writing. And personally, I am not so sure that I am all that good at it. Maybe the reason I don't think I am really all that good at it is because at one time I was convinced that I wasn't supposed to be doing it.

I eventually convinced myself that I was not supposed to enjoy anything. No one ever really told me that...I just... guessed. So when someone told me that I had drawn a "good picture" I was inwardly driven to say "no it isn't". If a teacher told me that a "write up" was "really good" I was inwardly compelled to trash it. I refused to believe that I could do anything good. Because, as far as I could tell, I wasn't any good.

Part of me wanted to be good enough, to believe that I could do "something"...anything "good enough". But another, stronger part of me "knew" that there was no way I could ever be "good enough". How could I do anything "good enough" when it was so obvious in so many ways that I wasn't "good enough"?

One day in sixth grade I stumbled across a big word in a Social Studies Light Unit that described me to a "T" and at once solidified and smashed a hundred or more beliefs I had about myself. The word, was *illegitimate*. "So that is the big, deep dark fact about me" I thought as I sat there in my desk. I was angry, confused, and miserable. I went on with school lessons and normal school life, because, well...who would care? A mixture of self hatred and God questioning raised their heads and began to take root and spread inside me.

I was sure I was bad, and there was no way I could do anything good enough for anyone to like me. I knew that no one could like, let alone love me. I did not even bother considering whether or not God could.

Fast forward to high school. Twelfth grade. By that time I had home schooled two years...but tenth through twelfth grades found me back in school.

There was a teacher...

Steve was everything I wished I could be and...wasn't. He was a couple of years older than I was and knew his stuff. And knew how talk and how to write, both of which I desperately wished I could and hopelessly knew I couldn't do. And he encouraged me to write.

I was told I worshiped him and that I tried to copy him. Whatever I tried to do by way of improving how I did things was "copying" and therefore not really who I was. In short, trying to be like Steve drove me to be fake. At least that is what I was told.

One afternoon, since I was done with my school work for the day, I took a pen and paper and began to write something that had been "growing" on me. I am not sure how much I wrote but, it was a lot. I wrote as if I was inspired. Since I was in typing class at the time, I used some of my spare time in typing practice typing out this article.

Meanwhile...

I kept getting what I thought were signals that I was not supposed to be writing. Anything. I was told that I was showing off, which may have been partially true. I was accused of trying to look like something I actually wasn't, which may have been partially true.

Any attempt to write caused tension at home. I was showing off and did not have any good motives for trying to write, I was told. Life became so unbearable that I did the only thing that made sense to me.

I made a private, inward promise to myself to do absolutely no writing, of course outside of what I had to do for school.

And something inside me died.

Life at home began to go a little better, actually, after I made this vow to myself. Then one Saturday there was a flare up of conflict. It may or may not have had anything to do with whether or not I did any writing.

One of the Saturday chores was burning the trash. As I was gathering the trash, I was fuming. Things were going to get worse before they promised to get better. I gathered all the manuscripts of anything I had written...typed and in my handwriting. I stuffed it all in the trash bag I was collecting the household trash in, and hauled it all out to the burn pile.

And it went up in white smoke.

Meanwhile to "Up in White Smoke"

There was a nursery just up the road from where we lived. The owners were longtime friends of our family. Some of my older siblings worked for the Noyses. One afternoon when I was in tenth grade they needed someone to help load a truck to ship somewhere.

After it was done, I offhandedly said "I would be kind of interested in working here."

They came over a few days later, and I began an extended part time job that lasted until I was twenty-two.

Squaw Mountain Gardens was a haven in a chaotic teen life. It was where I slowly began to grow up. It was a place to productively let out a little bit of my nervous, angry, insecure energy. It was a place to take a few baby steps toward independent thinking.

It was a place to escape...temporarily...from living under dad's thumb. But I could not understand why my bosses at work expressed confidence that I could work this job and learn new things while apparently...a quarter mile down the road, and around the sharp curve we lived on...I couldn't do anything right.

One afternoon, my boss said they were going to come over sometime and bring something for me that they thought I could use. I had no idea what to expect. I had no idea how it was going to affect my life.

One rainy morning they showed up...with their old desktop computer. I was stunned. Never mind that it was on the old side. Or that I would have to start at the bottom of learning how to run the thing. Or that I barely knew how to type.

This was after I had trashed all the writing I had done, including some poetry. This was after I had taken the private, inner vow to not ever write again. This was after I had destroyed one of the manuscripts I had written.

Did I mention that I was stunned?

I stammered my thanks...my shock and surprise was all over my face.

It wasn't until a number of years later that I realized that this was God's way of saying that writing was okay. That it was part of what He wanted me to do. Later I would wrestle through questions like how can something I enjoy possibly be good...let alone God's will? Wasn't it just a "dumb hobby"? I could not imagine it ever being good for any thing. I didn't know. I really had no idea.

I barely believed in God...much less thought He was good. I did not have a "relationship" with Him. I was a member of a Conservative Mennonite Church...although I was not born again when I "joined church" and was "baptized" with a handful of water.

The tortuous path that marked my path to God and faith and salvation is another long story...which is for another time.

Chapter 12

So it seems
You were saying all along
That where I am's not really
Where I belong.
My heart will
Never really settled be
As long as others
Call the shots for me.
I've allowed men's will
To override your plan
Tried to convince myself
I've done the best I can.
What have I gotten?
Just an empty,
Wayworn heart...
Full price of turning back
From what You showed me
From the start.
I may never
Fully get back to that place...
Get another feeling
Of your sweet embrace...
But I've learned lessons
From the times
I was forced to seek your face.
One thing I've learned
Is that you can't
Earn grace.
JPB

It would be kind of a nice Christmas gift to Jesus to let Him come into my heart.

I thought I was sensing "the voice of the Spirit" in my heart. Some of my friends were already "becoming Christians". The peer pressure was rather strong. So was the desire for whatever they were finding as they "came to Christ."

So why didn't I? The answer is simple…painful…and true...

You really don't know what you are doing. I was protected from the "false commitment" that child evangelism would have led me into. But where I felt myself driven to far out weighed any harm that would have come from child evangelism.

I was twelve years old, and it was close to Christmas. I thought about it for a while, without saying anything to any one.

Then came the Wednesday evening before Christmas vacation. I slipped mom a note in the van at church after prayer meeting, that said "I want to become a Christian."

Mom said that they would talk about it. Dad got into the van soon after, and we left for home.

Several nights later, after family devotions, we sat down and began talking about it.

"Why do you want to become a Christian?"

I did not know how to say the "right answer" I just knew... what they thought about Child evangelism. Would this look too much like it? Plus I had a paralyzing fear of not saying the right thing. I am almost sure mom and dad did not intend to put impossible pressure on me.

I froze. Literally, I could not say a word.

For several agonizing minutes we sat there in silence. The blood throbbing in my ears.

Finally dad cleared his throat. It was over.

I could not...or would not say what I was thinking or feeling or what I knew. It was clear that I did not understand what "becoming a Christian" meant.

I was told to wait until I knew what I was doing.

So we got up and went to bed.

I felt like I was turned away from Jesus. By the ones I hoped...or thought...or expected...to be able to lead me to Him. By the people much smarter and wiser than I would ever hope to be...my parents.

I am not sure what I hoped...or wished...or longed for. Something...that mom and dad would have been able to say to me or do for me. It didn't take long to figure out that mom and dad couldn't give me what I needed (although they probably would have tried to if they could have...if I could have brought myself to put it into words.)

Are there words for something that hurts so much you scream for relief from it and yet you feel compelled to thrust it, and the ones who could give you relief from it, away from yourself?

At this point, the inner, trained, uncomfortable with pain and honesty "I have the answers to all of your questions" part of me begins jockeying for attention...and I have to tell it to shut up...for now.

It is like trying to put a bandage on a wound while the blood is flooding out of it. All of this is kind of like the blood and toxins coming out after being held in for years. After the bleeding stops it will be time for healing creams and bandages and the rest of it.

When are you going to know when to put the bandages on?

I don't. I am not going to put any bandages on. Neither are you.

But you need a doctor.

The Doctor is here. He has been here all the time. His name is Jesus.

Someone is going to be horrified that I refer to the inner me as an it.

The literalistic are gonna have a cow over some of what they just read.

Let 'em.

How many times do I have to remind myself that I am not writing this for literary critics, or to for those who wish I would just sugar coat everything?

So...the messiness here only means that I walked in on...a spiritual surgery?

Yes, that is right...you walked in on the wound cleaning, and the bandaging.

Is it okay if I stay here?

It is if it is okay with Him (motioning to the Great Physician)

Just be quiet and listen...you might miss something if you pepper us with a lot of questions.

I have no idea what my teen years might have been like had I been "allowed" to come to Jesus.

So, should I wish things would have been different?

I do, but should I?

I do not know.

That is my answer to a lot of things.

I do know what my teen years were like.

I became a silent rebel. I "stuffed" everything until something "set me off" and I would "explode" at the most inconvenient times. And it was often for the most unconnected things.

Unexplainable anger.

Indefensible tantrums.

Irrational actions.

Like...throwing tools. One time I actually threw a rake at dad, and it ended up broken and we had to fix the rake.

Or...acting out in a rebellion at school that mainly resulted in chaos for a few days at school and being forced to mutter a forced, public apology in front of every one.

Or...flying into a rage of frustration over not being able to "get" algebra.

Or...fantasizing about suicide...and knowing in the next instant that it wouldn't really do any good.

Or...thrashing the thistles and tansy in the back half of our property with almost totally frustration and anger fueled energy.

Or...having the nervous, angry, adrenalin charged energy to chop and stack large amounts of wood...while we still used wood for heat.

The prediction that I was going to have a turbulent teen age began to be fulfilled. And as far as I was concerned, no one really cared.

You could describe me in three words.

Angry.
Confused.
Sad.
Angry at what? Confused about what? Sad about what?
I had no idea.

*An awkward kid
In the back edges of the crowd
With a full head of curly hair.
A scared feeling in his heart:
"I hope He doesn't notice me—-
Yet wish He would"
Is written all across his face.
He doesn't really trust his own mom
Hardly even knows his dad.
He doesn't even know
Why he is here.
Someone said
Jesus was a kind and gentle man...
Almost fun to be around.
And it sort of looks like He is.
But those twelve men—-
They say they're called disciples—-
They're big and strong...important.
You would have to be...
To be a friend of Him.
He looks around
And sees his friends
Around the master.
He's just about to move
And make his way up to the Man...
But Peter, James and John
Push him away.
"Look here, Jesus is busy
And has no time for you.
Don't you know that He's been teaching
All day long?!"
The moms of some of his buddies*

Anxiously pull their sons away
Fully accepting the disciples word
That their kids were in the way.
Those closest to the Master say it
So of course it must be true.
Cause look, he's not too smart,
Is shy in crowds...
Often clams up when spoken to
Especially by the important...
Which the Twelve are, certainly.
There is no way a little kid his age
Could understand
The deep and profound things
The Lord has had to say.
The disciples' rebuke is suddenly
Put to silence by a look
From the Master they professed
To Follow and protect
From the grimy, sticky hands
Of untrained kids.
"Allow the children—
Bring it on. And don't you dare
Forbid them."
The disciples—shocked, bewildered;
The children; overjoyed...
Can they believe it...
And can they actually come...
And will He actually accept them...
They're not really in His way?
Some race up through the crowd
To be the first to scramble
Onto His lap.

But some hold back,
And they can hardly help it...
Been told so long
They are not worth His time.
They gasp and almost fear to believe it
Can childish hearts and hands
Reach up to the Divine?
He bids them "Come"
And some of them start coming...
This Kingdom of God
Thrives on such as these...
With no more sense
Than to accept His offer
With shrieks of joy
Scramble up on His knees.
The kingdom of God
Is far from "adult wisdom"
It's in a child now laughing on His knees.
   JPB

We were practicing for a Christmas program.

I was in seventh grade. One of my friends and I were cutting up all through practice. (Our school was in the basement of the church. We were practicing in the auditorium.) I do not remember what I did that got me in trouble...but I had to stay after school.)

I sat on one of the benches in the entry way attempting an "I don't care...you aren't going to tell me anything" pose. It worked for a while. The teacher came up and sat beside me and started talking about "don't you want to become a Christian?" I finally prayed a halfhearted prayer to get her off my back.

Whether my teacher actually thought I really had become a Christian and really had given Jesus my heart, I don't know.

I was finally able to go home. Some school friends were over, and I soon got involved in a game of hide and seek in our house.

I assumed my teacher said something to mom and dad about why I had to stay after school. I guessed she told them that she had talked me into praying and asking Jesus into my heart.

If I was supposed to tell them, I didn't. If I was supposed to say I wanted to join the instruction class, I didn't.

I knew too much.

Fast forward to a certain Sunday morning not long there after.

Intermediate class. At least eight or ten of us almost teenagers.

Senior, the teacher that year, decided to ask us if we were "born again."

Most of the others were able to say yes.

Too soon it was my turn.

"Are you a Christian, Josh?"

Gulp.

Burning red ears.

Wildly throbbing heart...that might be said to be "conviction".

"Um"

(shuffle of feet)

"No."

"I'm praying for you, Josh."

Shame.

Inner confusion...burning condemnation.

I was forced to look like a fool in front of my friends...again. I was certain I looked really, really stupid...bad...a thousand words...yet no words could have expressed how I felt.

It was...too much like that night I couldn't say why I wanted to "become a Christian".

Senior moved on to the next one. Finally.

The first and second bells rang.

Finally...the unendurable...almost eternal class was over.

We escaped. To the relative safety of the hallway and then made our way to the auditorium upstairs.

One morning I got to school and walked in on a couple of my friends trying to look up something in the Bible.

"Oh, here comes Josh...ask him where it is."

Huh? What?

I was far from thinking I was a Bible Know it All. Or any other sort of know it all. I was far from thinking I was even smart. I would have assured you I thought I was stupid. As far as I could tell, everything proved I was. Such as the fact that everyone finished my sentences. Everyone knew I wasn't much good at running games. In short, I was a ten-second kid in a two-second world.

And incredibly, I came across as a know-it-all.

I could not imagine why they thought I was a walking Bible Answer Book. As far as I knew, I didn't know too much... about anything.

So...I was a know-it-all, an awkward know it all, a keep everything to yourself know it all.

At least sometimes.

I was desperate to protect myself.

From something that I could not even name.

I did not even knew what it was.

I had shut and locked the doors to it too many times to be able to get back there without help. Help that I was unable, and unwilling to ask for.

Because...who would care?

I swung between saying I was a Christian to claiming I wasn't. My inner life did not make any sense to me, and I am sure it did not make any sense to any one who looked on.

How could it have made sense? Does it make any sense to be pushed to the brink of cracking mentally by unattainable demands? Like the many mornings I had to "put on" a "school face" to hide the pain of the morning.

Then came the spring that I was seventeen. Revival meeting time came around as it did every year.

The evangelist who came veered a little too close to child evangelism...for my folks liking. I had that sense...or whatever you are supposed to call it...several times before then. Conviction...often said to be signaled by your heart beating a little bit faster...maybe your palms getting a little sweaty... Being convicted by the Spirit so that you had no peace and couldn't really even sing the invitation song after the sermon.

Unless you went forward.

Which I didn't. So I never had peace because I never went forward. I do not know what would have happened had I gone forward. I knew I would go forward, kneel at the front bench, and then...

What?

The same thing that happened that long ago night when I was twelve, for all I knew.

It went the same as always. The sermon. The invitation. The wildly beating heart. The sweaty palms. The being almost unable to sing the invitational song.

The song ended.

We stood for closing prayer.

And were dismissed.

After dismissal we stood around talking.

My older brother, who was also the deacon at church at the time, came over to where I was standing.

He said a few words...and I don't even remember what they were.

I do remember that it resulted in me finally getting to my knees. Mom and dad and were apparently motioned to the front.

Dad said to my brother "Why don't you lead him into it?"

So he did.

We prayed, confessing the sins that I could think of, asking for forgiveness and so forth. We got up and I was declared a new creature in Christ.

We went home eventually. Several people congratulated me for giving my life to Christ.

In bed that night I tried to convince myself that what had happened was true. I tried to drum up a sense of "assurance of salvation".

The sense of assurance that was supposed to come...didn't. And I didn't know why.

Maybe I wasn't really born again? Maybe there was something in the way that I did not know...or was ignoring?

The next day was the first day of being a "new creation in Christ". And to be honest, I did not really know what I was supposed to do...much less how I was supposed to feel.

Because I felt no indication that anything had changed in me.

That night they asked for testimonies. So, mostly because it was expected, when it seemed to be my turn I stood to my feet. I read a verse from First John and stammered what I hoped would sound like a "testimony" was supposed to.

Thus began what was supposed to have been my walk with Christ.

The year or so between that night and baptism was a year of wondering...of doubts...of getting a head full of facts and an increasingly emptier, if not heavier heart.

And, somehow, I was allowed to go through instruction class.

I say that, because there was no proof or fruit of repentance in my life.

I had little or no peace. The times I had a sliver of "assurance" were few and far between. It was nearly impossible to control the anger and rage that brewed just below the surface and often boiled explosively to the surface.

The Friday before I was baptized, we were playing softball at school. (It was May, during 12th grade) The third baseman/shortstop had thrown me out. I angrily flung him to the ground in retaliation. The entire school saw it.

I was the oldest one in school, so it made quite a scene.

I later went back and asked his forgiveness.

So...we bought a suit and made the coat over into a plain coat. I am not sure I ever really had what is called a "conviction" for the plain coat. I was primarily lunging for an identity.

I was desperate to fit in...somewhere...for any reason.

So...although it doesn't make much sense to me now, getting that suit coat made over in time for the Sunday of baptism was a big deal.

I have wished since then that I had had the honesty to... even in the last minute...to back out of receiving the handful of water that was poured on my head that morning.

But, I didn't.

I did not have the freedom to ask questions. I do not mean permission bestowed by parents or authorities. I am talking about what I will call "inner permission".

Chapter 13

Life seems to teach
You have to be just right
To have a chance
In anybody's sight.
It's not enough
To be just simply me
What others think
Keeps me from being free.
Then why does life
Seem pointless, if so lived?
Eye pleasing fails
In what it tries to give
It often takes
Too long, this truth to learn:
Our hearts are made
For greater things to yearn.
An empty heart,
A pride enshrouded soul
Jesus, I bring
And long to be made whole.
Savior, your hands
Were crushed, for love of me.
You've won my heart
And I am finally free.
JPB

The (unlikely) road to voluntary service

I home schooled in seventh and eighth grade. I could admit that I could not stand my seventh grade teacher. I could admit that I had such dislike for her that at the end of seventh grade I was begging...literally...to home school. And when I heard that she wasn't teaching again, a couple of years later, I begged just as much to go back to school.

It was during these two years that I "became a Christian" and joined church. I could talk about the last two years of school and the two terms of Bible School I attended in Missouri.

I could talk about a lot of things, and they would all fit in to the narrative of the unlikely road that led to voluntary service.

When I got out of school I was working part to full time at a nursery. My goals in life: get out of school, maybe get in a term or two at Bible School, get the nerve to send something to a publisher, maybe once...If that was possible.

Beyond that, I was pretty much directionless.

I am not really sure what I expected out of Bible School. I went under the impression that you were supposed to go looking somehow "victorious" or "mature" or something that I knew I wasn't.

I remember hearing "how do you expect to get anything out of Bible School if you are such an emotional and spiritual mess here at home?"

I didn't know. I don't even remember my given reason for wanting to go to Bible School. My two terms of Bible School can be described as long on the books and short on relationships. I had to get good grades. I was deathly afraid of becoming one of those Bible school kids who got into trouble and got sent home.

That last sentence makes me laugh. Or cry. Or some of both. I was absolutely no good at volley ball...which was the activity of the afternoon after last classes. At that stage of life if you were good at volleyball...you were...good.

Anyone could play volleyball better than I could. Anyone could do anything better than I could.

I inwardly mocked at all the guys and girls who "only came to Bible School to find their life partner." And took pride in the fact that I wasn't about to do any such shallow beside-the-point-of Bible-school thing.

I didn't. Instead, I returned home from Bible School prouder and with a lot more knowledge. And I was a lot more hollow.

I tried to pass for more mature than I was. I tried to come across as knowing more. Maybe I did.

It was all empty and futile and pointless.

I was actually less secure. I now knew a lot of kids from a lot of different places...and compared to what I saw of their lives, mine sucked.

I was very discontent...I knew people who had been "all over". I had been out of the country maybe once or twice.

Almost every one I knew had their own cars...or trucks. I didn't have a car.

I couldn't even drive.

Thus my two terms at Bethel Bible School came and went. The afternoon I got back from Bible school I was out checking fence on our property. I wondered what the point of the previous three weeks was...and hopelessly rebelled against the pointlessness of coming back to...this.

My return back home from Bible School after my second term coincided with grandma B. moving in with us. She had actually moved in a week or so before.

We were doing supper dishes. I was washing and grandma was rinsing. I missed a spot or something on a dish...or maybe a piece of silverware. That sparked a disagreement that led into an argument that flung me into a tantrum and her into a rage.

And I wished, among other things, that I could die.

What did Bible School do for you? Apparently...nothing.

I was irrationally...almost helplessly...angry. Always. I did not even know why, entirely. Home life was almost unbearable at times. Life was more or less pointless. My job at the nursery was the same sort of escape that school had been.

As far as I knew everything that was wrong was my fault.

Fittingly enough, that got me nowhere.

"Did you hear who is going to Belize?"

"I just heard someone else is going to Romania."

"Hey, did you hear who is dating?"

"Are you going to their wedding?"

Somehow, I hated hearing news like this. Everyone else was going into service, teaching school, dating, getting married. "Living the dream."

Meanwhile...I was twirling my fingers around in nursery potting soil. I didn't hate my job at the nursery. I had held a job there for several years and knew all the ropes. There was a future to be had in the nursery...if I would have wanted it.

I wanted it..but I didn't. I was bored and wanted something more, without even knowing what that something was.

One day I got a letter from a Bible school friend. He was planning to go to work in Virginia. Harrisonburg, Virginia. Christian Light Publications, to be precise.

Later we talked on the phone.

I flopped on my bed, staring up at the ceiling. It all seemed pointless. I could see no future to look forward to.

Would it be possible to be "good enough" to be in service... in Virginia...or anywhere? The chances of that ever happening seemed so remote as to be laughable.

The thought slipped me into a quiet, hopeless depression.

It quietly ate at me that everyone was able to do all the things I couldn't.

I was angry at life, at myself, and at God. I was jealous of any one who seemed more fulfilled and successful in life than I was.

I was also furious at someone I wasn't even aware of.

One afternoon I took mom aside and told her I was thinking about going into voluntary service...somewhere.

By the next afternoon, several fingers on my right hand were crushed in a metal roller because of an act of total stupidity on my part.

For a few months, at least, any ideas about service were pushed into the back ground and forgotten.

It soon became clear that I was not voluntary service material. We were fixing up Grandma's property in Salem, trying to get it ready to sell. So, with bandaged right hand and maybe some mild pain killers, I tried to pull my share of the load.

And grew more and more irritated at myself for how stupid I had been.

It didn't help that around that about a year later my brother, who owned the shop, got his foot crushed under one of the coils as he was attempting to load it one morning.

I began to think maybe I cursed everything I touched.

After a few phone calls to CLP, it became clear that I was not going there any time soon.

One day mom made what struck me as a stupid suggestion.

"I think you should go to Faith Mission."

I was so determined to go to CLP that I let the idea pass from my mind. And waited for a call that would indicate that CLP had changed their mind...or something.

Thus passed a long, rainy fall and winter.

Nothing could have prepared me for what was just around the corner.

Chapter 14

(Fetal Alcohol Spectrum)

Sometimes forbidden information is what it takes to give you the first clue toward understanding yourself. Especially if that information is so much like a mirror that it is almost scary. And also especially of you are more or less prevented from knowing about it...because "you might take it wrong"...it really adds to the mystery...and intrigue when you are actually told what it is.

I have always known my parents were alcoholics...and it was vaguely rumored that it has somehow affected me. But it never really went much further than just a rumor...and it no one ever really connected the dots.

Fetal alcohol exposure is basically what happens when a pregnant mother drinks alcohol (in any amount) during her pregnancy. It can have severe, sometimes almost invisible effects on the child.

As it usually seemed to happen, another family in our church had found out about someone who had done some research of some sort on the effects of alcohol on families, or something.

So, there was a meeting of the church parents one evening to listen to this lady...mostly to see if there was anything to her claims on the subject.

Apparently there was...at least in relation to the other family. And for some reason, that I am still not sure I understand, it apparently suddenly clicked, at least mom said it did with her.

What she was hearing about this thing called fetal alcohol began to sound a lot like me, apparently.

Meanwhile, I had spent most of my teenage years wishing and not wishing by turns that I could somehow find out what on earth was making me be the mess I was.

Why was I so far from normal, and yet so close to it and yet so far from it that I was treated like I was normal and abnormal...and a lot of the time driven to feel as if I was actually retarded?

So, any sliver of a reason...even if it was a bad one, or would make me feel even more terrible about myself, or worse about my real parents...or anything...would have been better than having to carry the weight of being different, "slow" or mildly retarded, for no visible or invisible reason.

So when mom and dad sat me down a few nights after this meeting, the facts they told me were prefixed and suffixed with "none of this is meant to give you an excuse for being the way you are."

I silently thought, "well, if you are afraid you are giving me an excuse, why are you bothering to load me up with this?"

I didn't say that, of course, because I knew better than to say a lot of what went through my mind.

I sat there in the living room, listening to mom read a lot of information and lots of lists about the effects of alcohol on the unborn, and how the effects would go on throughout life. And how the condition somehow compensated for the damage it caused, and other things. For the first time in my life I actually could almost understand why I was the way I was.

But I was told this was not supposed to be an excuse.

That totally made no sense to me. It was like finally being handed a mirror...I finally had a tiny way to understand why my mind worked (or sometimes did not seem to work) the way it did.

So that is why I...a million things about me began to make sense.

I mean no disrespect when I say that I could not figure out why mom seemed to think my knowing all this might be a bad thing somehow.

It helped explain...kind of...why I have never really felt comfortable behind the wheel of a car. For a long time I assumed, and had been told that I apparently did not want to drive (which was/is absolutely not true). I could throw all sort of blame around, such as that I had almost no behind the wheel time before I took drivers ed...and failed the behind the wheel part of the course. I assumed it was something about me...again. I was too dumb to be able to put into practice behind the wheel what I had apparently grasped in my head... and inexplicably passed the classroom part.

There are jokes about parents getting twitches or close to heart attacks from teaching their children to drive.

Apparently I was supposed to just know how to drive without ever getting behind the wheel...never mind my poor hand eye coordination, and lacking distance judging abilities, and a host of other things.

So when one evening sort of off handedly, mom and dad said, as they were heading out the door to go some place "you can get your drivers permit if you want."

I was all of 19.

Probably still considered as much of a retard as ever, for all I knew...

19.

I am more or less embarrassed to admit what age I was.

So I got my permit one Friday afternoon.

It is a strange phenomenon to live in a household where you are treated as if you are too stupid to make any decisions on your own and then all of a sudden dumped into a situation where you are expected to act the age you are...eighteen or nineteen, as was the case.

Dad and I stopped by the DMV on the way down to Salem, where we were helping grandma get ready to move up to Estacada with us.

I got my permit and then we went on down to Salem.

I knew instinctively there was no point in asking dad if I could drive. The answer would have been a no, I am almost certain. I had barely been allowed to back the van out of the carport, let alone out the drive, and for sure NOT on the road.

I am not sure where I was expected to get any know how about driving, I really got next to no practice. Mostly because my attempts behind the wheel made mom so tense and impatient that I tensed all up and my confidence drained to below zero.

My few attempts to drive were more or less disasters. No one got hurt, and nothing got damaged, but I underwent enough trauma that I almost dreaded the idea of trying to drive anywhere.

On the way back from Salem that night, about midnight, I was asleep in the passenger seat.

As we came close to Estacada on the "New Highway 224", apparently dad was asleep as well.

We both awoke about the same time, going full speed ahead in the grass on the opposite side of the four lane highway than we should have been on.

I do not know why we were the only traffic on the road at that moment. If there would have been traffic on the road, we might have both been killed.

I spent the next several days wondering why we hadn't been and I half wished that we had been.

After a go or two at the wheel, it was decided that I go out on the road with dad. We were going to go to somebody's place a few miles up the road. Me, with next to no experience, and dad, with next to no inclination to tell me what to do. So he pretty much sat there and watched.

Which I guess might have been a tiny bit better than being chewed out for every single mismove until I was almost too shaken and too close to paralyzed to be able to function, let alone drive.

Besides, I found driving with all the things that were involved...mentally tiring. I was actually exhausted by the five mile drive to or from church.

Having eyes that were incredibly sensitive to light did not help, especially at night. And having siblings that were better than good at pretty much everything they did (so it seemed to this loser, who almost could do nothing right two times in a row) and rubbed it in at every opportunity, and made known that they were able to do it, so could I, you have proved you could do it by the fact you can do this, this and the other thing.

What would have been the point of saying I can't...as in physically can't do certain things? It would have been attributed to my simply not wanting to...or the fact that I was simply too bitter (thank you so very much for that insight.) If it is so true, and if you have such glowing insight, maybe you could show me how to get deliverance from it. Oh, really? You smash me with condemnation and leave me feeling shamed and stripped and powerless to do anything about it...and refuse to point the way...or even try to understand (not that you could)...and go on your own self righteous way, sure that you were the voice of God that this jerk should have listened to...because it was soo clear you told the truth. Yes...you did, and spoke more death than life into my spirit.

That is more or less the way the conversations that went on...or would have gone on had I opened my mouth on the subject. If one of my siblings, or someone so obviously more spiritual or in control said something that was right...totally right...and if I did not match up to it...I was the rebel, the one who was in the wrong, the one who wasn't listening to God.

The one who was so stupid he had to be controlled by spiritual abuse to the point of not being allowed to see or try to get free from it without dire consequences.

Which one day, despair and an almost insane quest for truth drove me to.

Meanwhile, with almost no behind the wheel time, I tried for my license, three different times.

And, perhaps predictably, failed each time.

Maybe it was the lack of practice...maybe.

Maybe it was my attitude toward God and others about... everything.

Almost certainly it had nothing to do with any of the things we had been finding out about why I am the way I am physically. That would have been too...easy, maybe?

It would have explained too much, and yet opened the door to too many questions.

I was not quite told "here are the facts, but ignore them..." but it came close to that.

I got very conflicting messages.

So one afternoon I had an appointment at the eye doctor in Estacada. It almost went the same way as it did several years before. Except that the girl who was doing the exams and running the tests was just a bit too talkative and friendly.

We got talking and for some reason I blurted out that I was adopted. I had no idea why I said it.

It turned out that she was too, or something. Then I mentioned something that I had no reason to bring up...I mentioned that my parents were alcoholics or something, and also something about this thing called fetal alcohol that supposedly might have something to do with my eyes or something.

She said "I have heard about that." She entered some information into her computer there in the office and apparently got some data that changed things.

In a couple of weeks, I was wearing glasses.

At first they were just reading glasses, and it was sort of on a "try this and see if this works" basis.

It did for a while.

After a while I realized that the close up reading lens were not really helping with distance vision. So it was off to the eye doctor, again.

This time they fitted me out with progressive lenses, and it was also my first pair of "self darkening" glasses.

My headaches began to leave...I thought. At least they occurred less frequently. Instead of almost every day nearly, they came around about once a week. I could almost tell when they were coming on.

For the most part, the purpose of the lens is to literally force my eyes to focus together, since I have what might be called weak eye focus muscles. So, after a few days of being "forced" to do what the normally functioning eyes do...focus together...my eyes and the eye muscles literally rebel in pain.

When this happened, I could feel it from the back of my eyes to the pit of my stomach, it was almost as if everything in my was tied up in one tight wad.

Meanwhile, the lens that "forced" my eyes to focus also gave my face the appearance of an almost constant scowl.

Of course, this sounds like a huge excuse marathon... someone is going to say that I was extremely bitter...and they are right, partly. They are going to say you were as angry as you looked...and they are right, partly. They will say that I am trying to excuse myself...and they can think they are right if they choose.

One morning I went to the eye doctor, again. The doc looked at my prescription and almost had a hissy fit. "Did you know your prescription is so strong it literally overcorrects?"

Um, yeh, I knew that. That was the idea...to force my eyes to focus...even if it compelled me to wear a perpetual scowl, and opened the door to almost constant misunderstanding.

"You need a prism in the left lens."

"Um, ok...what will that do?"

He told me in some technical jargon. But after a year or so of a prescription that had frankly not really worked, I was ready to try something else.

However the prism does it, it works.

I still get headaches...sometimes severe...but rarely as frequently...for sure not every other day.

Chapter 15

You lost the script.
The words have changed.
And everything's
Been rearranged.
The props have dropped
And fallen flat.
Your show has crumbled
Just like that.
The world is watching
What will you bring:
Just some more empty words
Or the real thing?
There's reality
Beyond this set up show.
If you focus on the set
You may never know.
Is it solid or hollow:
Just how does it ring?
The lights in the eyes
And the smooth running show
May be hiding a life
Of scars too painful to know.
In a world of actors

*Is it any suprise
That the most successful
Fall apart
Or else dies?
At the top of his act
In the heat of his game
A tomb...
Now the limelight...
The heighth and the depth
Of his shallow, bright fame.
And the act...
Or the life...
Which of these
Will remain?
JPB*

It was somewhere around the first of January, 2000. I was fretting about if I would ever hear from CLP and if they would say yes and wondering if they would say why if they would say no.

It was a Wednesday, and mom and I were talking. We had arranged for someone to give us a call that afternoon, Eastern time.

Mom suggested for the second time: "I think you should consider calling Faith Mission."

I groaned inwardly.

Not Faith Mission! Not where they have retarded children… and you have to change diapers and…ugh! No, anywhere but there!

Out loud, I said "If CLP gives me a call and I get a no… (groan)…I will call Faith Mission."

The call came from CLP and confirmed that working there was a closed door. I mentioned that I was thinking about looking into Faith Mission.

The voice on the other end of the line, in Virginia, said he thought that would be a good idea.

So I hung up the phone. I sat drumming my fingers on the dining room table.

I picked up the Mennonite directory and thumbed through it to the Beachey Amish section. I found the name Faith Mission Home. I saw a name and a phone number to call.

Dennis Eash. Administrator.

I dialed the number and waited.

The number that was listed was actually Dennis' house, and his wife answered.

After briefly explaining what I wanted and getting the number to the main home, I hung up.

This is getting crazier by the minute.

Heart racing, I dialed, and waited.

The secretary answered and put me through to Dennis.

A half hour or so later, I knew where I was going to go. What I didn't know was how long it would take to actually get there.

Several days later a thick envelope with my name on it arrived from Faith Mission.

I filled out the application, and mailed it.

The date I put on the application form and the agreement to abide by the FMH rules was January 13, 2000.

A year later, I arrived at FMH.

A year that was the hardest...most stretching...most painful in my life up to that point.

Plans were for me to go sometime in March...then April.

Then it was indefinitely called off.

I went into a "tizzy".

Every night I would pray the same prayer. "Please. God tell me if I am supposed to go to FMH." I even set a date. God, tell me by so and so if I am supposed to go. And to my chagrin I got a reply just before that date.

Wait.

What are you supposed to say to that?

It came to a climax one night. I had no words. I was out of faith, frankly. I remember kneeling by my bed.

Faithless. Hopeless.

Almost.

Silence.

Then...

It wasn't exactly an audible voice. And it wasn't exactly an inner voice either. But it was a voice.

"You have asked and asked and asked. Now, shut up and let me work."

Does God say shut up?

He did.

It was like a slap in the face to get that word. So, I shut up and fretted, and worried, and...

Waited.

That August the youth group went on a camping trip. I did one of the stupider stunts I have ever done. And yet I felt absolutely self righteous and proud of how righteous I was. Virtuous about how much trouble I got the ones who were playing cards into.

Cards.

I am amazed now how shallow, and narrow and, proud I was at the time.

I was assistant Sunday School Superintendent at the time. I was riding the crest of a wave of "doing the right thing and telling on the bad boys".

The Sunday morning after we got back from camping I had Superintendent duties and had devotions.

During breakfast that morning, I found out that plans were being made for me to go to FMH the middle of January the following year, 2001.

After church that morning, there was a meeting about how to deal with some of the ones who were being "rebellious" at the time.

Meanwhile I was getting angrier and angrier. I worked myself into a near suicidal rage more than once. That probably sounds incredible, but it was an understatement at best.

Things would come up and I would "fly off the handle" and the following ugly progression would occur almost every time.

First a wave of almost uncontrollable rage over sometimes insignificant things.

Then I would quickly slide into self condemnation...self cursing...all the way to wishing myself to hell.

One afternoon, during such a round, I actually felt the flames of hell around my feet. I could all but smell it.

I was in the middle of a self destructive, self abusive, self condemning tantrum.

Everything I believed about God said that He should have slapped me.

Punished me.

Condemned me.

Wrote me off.

Said I was finished.

He should have done anything but what He did.

He was silent.

I cannot describe how wrong that seemed in the middle of the moment. I was about ready to write myself off. I was on the verge of writing a letter to the powers that be at FMH, telling them I was not coming. I knew I could not go, I was too much of a mess. In too much of a confused, tormented state of mind.

I even began writing a draft of a letter that said as much.

I was not really sure why I was so...enraged.

I was inches from throwing everything away.

One afternoon, Mom commented, "How do you expect to be able to work with mentally handicapped children when you are so full of hatred and rage?"

I didn't know.

"You really need to forgive your mom."

WHAAAAAT?!

Call it whatever you want, a word of wisdom on mom's part, that was the first time the thought actually crossed my mind.

I fought the fact for a while. But you can hide...or run from the truth for only so long.

Then came the nearly all night spiritual fight that changed everything.

Chapter 16

Father, you've always worked things out before.
Father, I long to trust you more.
Although my faith is oft so weak
And my own way I often seek...
Father, I long to trust you more.
I do not doubt you led me in the past:
Through peace and calm, or chilling blast.
But to my sight it is not clear
Where you are leading me from here...
Still, Father, help me trust you more.
Father, you promise "afterward" to show;
Reveal what mystifies us so;
If my own weakness proves you strong,
Then all is right though all seems wrong...
Grant me your grace to trust you more.
JPB

Once in a while I house sat for my boss and his family when they were on vacation. It was the week of Thanksgiving.

Mom had been "hammering" the idea that I needed to forgive my biological mom. I was perfectly miserable.

Wednesday evening after prayer meeting our chorus practiced for several upcoming Christmas appointments the next month.

Mom and dad went home right after prayer meeting. Dad was still in a wheel chair as a result of a tree cutting episode, earlier that fall, in our back yard that resulted in him breaking his left wrist and left ankle.

Seeing dad laid up in an easy chair and having to get around in a wheelchair did not help my outlook on life at all. We had to heft his wheel chair up the church stairs every Sunday morning and evening. I knew too much about what was going on the Saturday that dad fell from the tree and...well...changed things forever.

I sensed that I was somehow blamed for the events that led up to the accident. Such as the way dad tied off the branch he attempted to cut. I instinctively wondered about what he was doing but also knew he would ignore any objections I would have raised.

I was the lone witness to what happened in those minutes. I was actually in the middle of it all...standing on the bottom rung of the ladder. The butt end of the branch swung around and struck me in the chest before it swung up and landed with a crash on the house roof. I saw the branch coming toward me in slow motion, and felt myself flung backward to the ground by the force. I also felt "something" snap. This, at the exact moment that dad was flung to the ground, less than ten feet away. The running chainsaw, with its 36 inch bar, still running, landed between us. But a somewhat irrational instinct bade me get to my feet and...I am not sure what I thought I would do next. That was when I saw dad on the ground. About that instant, mom and my younger brother came running.

Most of the rest of that day passed in a blur of trying to clean up the branch mess and attempting to ignore the growing pain in my back and neck.

All this was whirling in my mind that Wednesday evening before Thanksgiving. I had a hard time seeing anything to be thankful for.

And I was getting ready to leave for FMH in January.

We got through practice and my brother gave me a lift to the nursery....which was just up the road from home.

We pulled in and parked by the gate.

My brother turned off the ignition and we sat there in the dark.

We talked for a long time about a lot of things.

I felt as if I was standing in front of a stone wall. God stood right there as well, saying "It's up to you, buddy. If you refuse to forgive your mom, your walk with Me is over."

What are you supposed to do when God says that to you? What can you do....but give in?

Finally...after several hours of unendurable spiritual warfare, I was given the grace to utter the words. "Okay, God, I forgive my biological mom."

When I said those words, I felt like I had become a new person. I felt as if I had finally tasted what it was like to be born again. I felt like I had let go of everything that defined my life up to that point. I had "let go of the rope" and had every sensation of free falling.

The next day was Thanksgiving.

In the following weeks, I faced a huge problem. How was I supposed to contact my mom?

I tried to draft a letter, and got about a page written. Suddenly I felt blocked.

Get her phone number and call her.

Gulp. Okay.

After several calls and one or more dead ends, I got what was supposed to be my mom's phone number.

A day or two before Christmas, I made the call that my mom said made her day, and her Christmas.

Meanwhile, I was scrambling to pack and get ready to leave for Virginia.

Chapter 17

Never in a hurry,
Always, yet, on time
Flows the wondrous working
Of the will Divine
That through storm or tempest
Does unceasingly,
A compass unerring
Guide eternally.
As a stream unhindered
Flows upon its way,
Never running empty
Fuller grows each day;
So your will, O Father
Shown to me each day
Does not yield to hindrance,
But makes clear the way.
Blessed compass, guiding
My steps in the night
That directs my footsteps
When sight fails, or light.
It shall be my guardian
Through life's winding way;
My sure guide from straying
Points to God for aye.

So I was finally going to go to Faith Mission. The place I dreaded and wanted to go to at the same time. The place my older sister had gone and served at ten years or so previously. The place where everyone was probably more mature and grown up and spiritually stable than I ever thought I could be. The place where you had to change diapers. Where you had to work with "retarded children". The place I absolutely did not want to go, but it seemed everyone thought might be a good idea if I went. The place that I was not really even sure why they would want someone like me to come to work there.

I scrambled to pack all my belongings and put what I would be leaving at home into storage. I packed a box, a suitcase and a duffle-bag. And had a backpack.

I really did not know what to expect at FMH. I was not even sure why I was going.

But I had my plane ticket in hand, and had told the administration when I was flying in and everything was being arranged.

I remember the last afternoon at home. It was a typically mild January afternoon, comfortable in a light jacket. There were some blackberries growing in amongst the grapes we had in our garden and since mom said she would like if they would be cleared out I decided to take them on as I had other areas in the garden. I had worked for several years at the nursery up the road, so this was more or less old hat.

As I was out there, whacking blackberries, I also pondered leaving home and flying to Virginia. I do not know if I should have been excited or not to be flying all the way across the nation. I was excited, a little bit.

Probably no one will miss me when I am gone.

I know, your thoughts about yourself when going into something big like voluntary service ought to be...noble, full of vision of what God will do with you, a thousand things.

Not...No one will miss me.

But that was the color of my thoughts. In fact, that was the exact wording of my thoughts.

So I whacked some more blackberries and mulled on that fact...or what I believed to be a fact.

I think it was that evening mom broke the news that Jesse and Sonya were going to be going to begin a two or three year term as house parents at Oakridge Cottage, at FMH. Whatever that was.

That was interesting.

Pretty much everything was in readiness. I made a last round of checking to see if I had packed everything I wanted to take with me. And made totally sure, about ten or eleven times that my ID and airfare and all that important stuff was in my backpack/carry-on.

At the time, part of my daily evening chores was peeling and grinding carrots for dad to drink in the course of the day.

So my last act at home was peeling, grinding carrots.

At family devotions we had sort of an air cleaning session (strange, I know, but true). Dad and Mom asked and extended forgiveness for wrongs in the past. And dad gave his best attempt at a blessing on me in going to Virginia.

Dad was just back on his feet after the tree accident three months earlier. He and Matt were going to take me in to the airport for the early (6:00 AM or so, I think) flight out of Portland.

I do not remember telling very many people good bye. It was easier and made more sense to me to just...leave.

The next morning, early, dad, Matt and I loaded up my stuff and we took off down the road to Portland.

We got to the airport.

I got to the ticket counter and almost had to shell out $25 for one too many carry-ons. I either looked pitiable enough, or it was so early (it WAS pre 9/11) or it was a total misunderstanding on my part, but I was allowed to get by without a fee, whether or not I should have paid one. Maybe that agent actually was an angel, I have no way of knowing.

So we went though security and hung out at the gate. When the time finally came, we bade each other relatively awkward goodbyes.

I got on the plane and found my seat, which was by a window. I watched the crew below as they were loading the luggage and saw them load up mine.

I breathed a small sigh of relief. At least my luggage was coming.

I got a stick of gum out of my backpack and began to chew it. I was in no mood to put up with popping ears.

I am sure I looked quite a sight.

I was told I had to take my suit coat, and I did not have room in my luggage, so I wore it under the winter coat I had on.

I think the flight touched down in Denver and perhaps at another stop before flying into Richmond, VA, where I was supposed to meet the man I had talked to a number of times on the phone but had never met in person...Dennis Eash.

I remember waiting in the terminal waiting for the flight to Richmond. I was hungry, but was also afraid I would miss the flight. (I was a bundle of almost out of control nerves.) I decided to buy a quick snack.

It was warmer than I expected it would be, and so when I got to a convenient place, I shed the really in the way suit coat and just had on the coat, and felt a lot better.

We flew into Richmond and taxied into the gate and unboarded. I scanned the crowd and saw Dennis...and almost wanted to go back on the next plane to Portland.

He had...of all things, a goatee.

This shows how shallow my perspective of life and people was. Also, I grew up in a Mennonite church hearing it pounded into us that beards were almost an unnecessary vanity, and anyone who dared to wear a goatee was either worldly, not really committed to being separated from the world, not really a Christian, and for not really any other reason than that.

So...It was a huge "pill" to swallow to actually accept that this goateed man was actually a Christian, let alone the administrator of FMH.

It was the first of a long progression of huge "pills" I had to swallow.

I came across as insecure slash know it all slash everything else in the two hour trip from Richmond to the little spot in the road called Free Union and on up the mountain to the ridge where I knew not what awaited me. We rounded a corner and there it was, Faith Mission.

It was Saturday, and for supper, every Saturday night at the Home they served pizza, Dennis said. So I was looking forward to having some pizza.

We drove up to what they called Boys Staff. We unloaded my stuff and took it to my room. Whoever my room mate was, was gone for the weekend, for a funeral.

So I had the room to myself.

We drove up to the Main Home...(I am not able to express how much...fear...I felt in the moment I stepped into the entry for that first time.) I told Dennis I wanted to call home and tell my parents I arrived. It was after supper, and some of the staff were in the living room playing a game of foosball.

We were greeted by Jeff and Alex.

I was almost embarrassed to see my name on the welcome banner that hung on the wall, with a lot of signatures.

I could hardly believe anyone would actually welcome me...especially someone who they didn't know, especially if they knew anything about who I was, which honestly, in the moment, did not look like all that much.

We had to cross that living room to get to Dennis' office.

I was sure every one was staring...criticizing...watching...me.

With fast nervous and long strides I followed Dennis into what I was to find was the most feared room in the building: 304.

Right then, it seemed to be the only almost safe place on the premises.

I called home, told them I had arrived and (half way lied) told them everything was going well.

I was nervous enough I could have puked, but also hungry.

Dennis offered to bring me a bit of supper so this shy new guy would not have to face anyone yet. Which I was glad he did, I am not sure I could have handled having anyone watch me eat.

As I have said many times since, I was the furthest thing from being "voluntary service material".

But, there was no pizza left over from supper, so Dennis scrounged up something from the left overs in the fridge.

I ate, and then knew I had to go back out there where every one was.

Opening that big white door and stepping into the Home Living room was the hardest thing I had done up to that point.

I arrived at FMH sure of a few things. I was a good Mennonite who was very conservative, and sure that the way "we did things back home is THE ONLY WAY to do things." I knew the Beachy's were more or less "safe", otherwise why would my folks have ever suggested and supported me going there?

There was another group that had its origins in hell, judging from what I heard about them. They were church splitters, took away the "weaker, dissatisfied, carnal" members from Mennonite Churches and more or less wrecked communities wherever they "made inroads".

They originated in Pennsylvania, and one of their leaders was a converted hippie.

There were a few things about this group that were grudgingly admitted. But by and large they were a bad influence.

And I was certain I would never have to worry about meeting anyone like that at a safe place like Faith Mission.

Charity.

Home fellowship churches.

They were so obviously of the devil that it caught me totally off guard when...

I actually met some of them.

In fact, I was "forced" to work with a number of them.

One girl in particular received the full weight of my Mennonite ire.

I had only heard bad about Charity, and as far as I knew, the only appropriate response was outright shunning. (This, for those who do not know, means to avoid or refuse to keep company with. It is a religiously sanctionable snub. In fact, in some circles of the church I grew up in, it was considered Scriptural.) Nothing in my Conservative Mennonite upbringing had prepared me to work side by side with someone from what was declared a totally heretical group.

It was almost impossible to shun in a public place like the halls of FMH without it being noticed and talked about and having it cause a strain on relationships.

But I had to know if she was real or not. As painfully ridiculous as it looks to me now, it was totally necessary. I was driven to it by a need to know what the truth was about people of that sort.

Without realizing it, I was deeply questioning a lot of the teachings, and values, and, yes, even the denunciations that came as a matter or course from the Mennonite mindset.

So for six months, I treated her in the only way a religious jerk like I was knew how to. I snubbed her in the halls. I refused to look at her, much less talk to her.

At first some thought I was just painfully shy around girls, and this was partly the case. After a while it became clear to everyone what was going on.

Two things were happening at once, and I knew it, and it scared me, and yet began to liberate me. I began "coming out of my shell." I started to loosen up in ways that I could never have imagined possible.

I began to realize that the Mennonite view of Charity as I understood it was absolutely wrong. After about six months, during early June it began to dawn on me. She was more of a Christian than I was.

That realization was almost intolerable, and it came on the heels of another realization. I had to apologize to her for the frankly ungodly way I had treated her.

For a good conservative Mennonite, this was almost the same as denying the faith. I knew this, but I also knew I had to do what I had to do.

So one Saturday afternoon, I called her aside in the hallway.

I was still as awkward and shy and stammering as I ever was in talking to girls, any girls.

But I told her why I had been such a jerk.

It turned out that she pretty much knew why I had treated her the way I did.

I told her I had come to the conclusion that she was more of a Christian than I was, and asked her if she could forgive me.

She did. And things might have gone better between us (it stayed more or less strained/casual/cordial) except for one thing.

I could not bring myself to accept her forgiveness.

Finally, a year from the day, almost, since I signed the agreement to abide by the FMH guidelines, I was standing in the entry way at FMH. Hardly knowing why I was there. Hardly knowing what I was supposed to do with myself.

I was almost certain that everyone else that was there was better than I was...at pretty much everything.

So, timid, and unsure and terribly awkward, yet desperately wishing I could fit in with all these mature youth that I had fallen in with, for perhaps strange reasons, I attempted to act the exact opposite.

I remember that first Sunday. I was told I would meet Ivan.

Judging from my impression of Dennis when I met him, I had no clue what Ivan was going to be like.

I did not know he was the bishop of the church.

And the assistant administrator.

And that he had been "single staff" himself back in the day.

All I knew was that I was terribly shy in crowds and hated to stand in line waiting to shake hands before or after church.

And we had to stand in line and wait in line to shake hands with, not just Ivan, but also two or three other preachers. All of whom were probably sizing me up, and probably had known my sister Sonya when she worked there ten years or so before.

We stood in line, (us staff guys would walk down the hill to the church) and it was (gulp) my turn to shake hands.

I stammered my hello and awkwardly greeted him in the "correct manner".

And our glasses knocked each other.

I was very self conscious the way it was, and I am not sure I was able to hide it as well as I tried to convince myself I had.

They did what is called separate seating, men on one side and women on the other. And sang more or less perfect a cappella. I had been used to a cappella back home, but nothing this good.

And besides, I could not sing, as well as some of the guys who were sitting around me.

We got through the songs. I swung from not being able to believe my ears (how good it sounded) to raw jealousy (at how some of the guys could hit the low notes and hit them hard, and how some of the other guys could soar into the tenor notes). Then from across the aisle I heard several female voices singing the obligato. Which was rare back home, to even have one or two girls who could timidly sing that high on occasion, let alone Sunday morning in church.

I really, really, began to wonder if it was possible to fit in.

We got through Sunday school and church.

After dismissal, we stood around briefly, those around me introducing themselves and asking who I was.

One or two asked "Oh, you are Sonya's brother?"

"Yes."

I finally was able to escape.

As I glanced around the auditorium, I noticed a side door.

Cool. I do not have to go through the embarrassment of standing awkwardly in line and awkwardly shaking hand and awkwardly greeting preachers with an awkward "holy kiss".

So I didn't. I escaped through the side door and made my way to the main Home.

And we had lunch.

But first, I met Tom Abrams.

Or rather, tried hard to understand him....and tried really hard not to be afraid of him...and tried really, really, really hard to eat my lunch after I first met him.

I was, frankly, grossed out at the sight of him.

Someone said they were going to go pass out tracts somewhere nearby and asked if I wanted to go along. I was pretty much in no mood to hang out with a bunch of guys who I guessed would just sit around and stare at me and ask me questions about myself that I would have to come up with answers to that (I did not even bother to hope) would sound like I knew what I was talking about.

So, I went along with AK and whoever else was going to pass out tracts.

The temperature outside wasn't exactly cold, and it wasn't particularly warm, either. And so we stood around waiting for the others...there were not really all that many.

Duane asked AK, "So who is your friend?"

"This is Josh. He just came here as staff this weekend."
"Oh. Well, welcome to the hills."

Thus it began...I was really the last person I would have suggested to work at a Children's home. And it must have been obvious. It became glaringly obvious in the first several weeks.

We would sit around slicing and dicing churches and rules and why our churches were better than others, and whether or not a cappella was the only acceptable music and if rock music was bad and why it was bad and, colors of material, etc....

Everything, except what really mattered.

But we thought those things mattered hugely, in fact they were life and death spiritual issues.

What really did matter then, if those things didn't?

Probably none of us really had any idea. At least we had no idea how to express if we did know. None of us would have really had the nerve to say what "it: actually was.

So...awkward.

Trying to fit in.

Indulging in heady and hollow discussions of issues.

Oh, yeah, it was a children's home, after all, wasn't it?

Chapter 18

Father, 'tis dark, the path I cannot see
That leads to life and endless peace in thee.
My hand in thine is all that holds me fast
While wending through life's fearsome, stormy blast.
Father, 'tis dark, and fears bedim my eyes;
I try in vain to quell the rebel sighs
That in my soul unuttered rise to Thee,
Forgetting that Thou always watchest me.
Father, though dark it is, a light I see
That bathes my darkened soul: the light is thee.
Thou never saidst that I'd not walk in night.
Only in darkness Thou wouldst be my light.
Father, I know night is allowed by thee;
For were it never dark, I would not see
The light of Thy bright presence leading high:
Yea, when Thou seemest most far, thou art most nigh.
JPB

I am not sure if it is more appropriate to say that my first week at Faith Mission "bombed" or was a total "wipe out."

Monday morning I got up, showered and got dressed and made my way to one of the prayer rooms in the staff house.

That morning was orientation. Ivan took me on the grand tour of the premises in the red Olds that had a distinctive grinding sound in the steering when you turned a corner.

The tour passed in a blur and eventually the morning was over.

After lunch, I spent the afternoon learning how to stain trim.

They were remodeling and adding several rooms upstairs in the main home for the staff girls. I got there in time to help with some of the sheetrock and staining lots and lots of trim.

The next day was day one of my first train in with a group of boys:

The C boys.

And I was beyond a bundle of nerves.

Day one did not go too bad, which means it was not a one hundred percent disaster. For the train in, I spent the first day observing the CCW and his group, trying to remember and catch on to a thousand and one things that I was supposed to do and remember and lots of things escaped me as soon as I heard it.

The next day, I was supposed to function as the CCW and the regular CCW would tag along and observe and give suggestions.

The following day was my turn to float the group. Solo.

It wasn't bad. And it wasn't really good either.

It was the day that I earned the nickname that has not quite worn off to this day.

"Sarge."

I was...mean. Although I did not mean to be. It is true that I did act pretty much like a drill sergeant, and did not give any of the boys any rope. Because I thought that is what you were supposed to do.

In the course of the next several weeks, I trained in to float most of the remaining groups.

Including the terrible E's.

The E's were...

William

Jeremy

Danny

Nathan (for a while)

Derreck

Train in day was terrible. Their CCW was frustrated and so were the boys (poor guys). The C boys were easy in comparison to what you had to do with these awful E's.

You had to do almost everything for them.

This means, you had to shower them, which was right after breakfast, including helping them get dressed and undressed. You had to brush their teeth for them, you had to make sure they got to the bathroom in time or else get to spend the next fifteen to twenty minutes changing, cleaning up and putting them into clean clothes. Sometimes six or seven or eight times in one day.

Then there was juice break followed by the trek down the hill to the mail box, accompanying the Home Ec teacher.

Between then and lunch there were various activities and classes, including setting one of the tables for lunch.

After lunch, there were classes and other activities, and in general keeping the boys active and occupied.

We survived the train in, only one day this time, and then I was supposed to float them, solo.

The day was fine until right after breakfast.

Shower time.

I was sweating with frustration within the first ten minutes.

You really, really, really have to do everything for these kids! Gahhg! Everything!

We got through shower time...barely. We were actually late for juice break, which was at 10.

After a hurried juice break snack, I left the dining room for a couple of minutes, and when I returned...

William was gone.

I panicked.

I was...livid.

I hardly knew William. All I knew was that he was autistic, that he rocked all the time, hated when anyone forced their way into his world, and, now. Was. Gone.

And, I all but hated him for being the way he was.

But for right now, I was in total panic mode. I had been warned that William "might" run off. And that he "might" take off toward the staff house.

I did not want to accept the idea that he would have actually ran off down to the staff house.

I asked, desperately, "Has anyone seen William?"

"Nope."

The secretary paged over the intercom and soon everyone knew.

Someone mentioned, again, "He might have run off down to the staff house."

Groan. No, not really??!

Well, there wasn't really any option but to go down and look. I left the other boys in the group in the care of someone and dashed...almost flew...down to the staff house.

I looked through the downstairs rooms.

No William.

I thought I might have heard a noise. Upstairs.

I dashed upstairs.

There, in the dorm at the corner at the end of the hall, was William.

Surrounded by an array of cookies out of a box that one of the staff guys had gotten recently.

After my initial shock of seeing him actually in there, devouring cookies and laughing and rocking, I flew into the room, made him get to his feet (I do not remember if he was wet or dry), we made our way as fast as possible out the door, and up the two sets of stairs to the main home.

I was livid, and literally shaking with rage.

There was almost no way I would be able to get through that day.

It really was a wild day.

Jeremy wet and "filled his drawers" several times that day.

Finally, we came to the end of the day.

I was sitting in the mailroom, after supper, fuming about how terrible the day had been with the awful E boys.

"I am going to go in and ask to never, ever, have that group again!"

"As if that is going to happen." Someone replied. "For all you know, you might get to like that group yet."

"I doubt it."

I actually had to float the boys, more than once, after that terrible day.

In time, I came to almost like the boys.

The day came, several months later, when I realized that I actually wanted to have them under my care.

How do you describe the process of coming out of a shell? Especially when at the time you did not even know you were living inside a shell? You probably start at the beginning, as close to it as you can remember.

I found out that I would be getting trained in for night duty some week in April. Night duty. Laundry for almost forty children. Washing laundry, drying laundry, folding and putting away laundry, hourly bathroom trips for certain of the boys.

Ugh.

I did not exactly hate night duty, and I certainly did not like most aspects of it. I did kind of like the idea of being able to be by myself.

There were a lot of things I was not counting on.

Like being on Night Duty during a thing called Former Staff Weekend.

And a boy named Nathan.

I was maybe two or three nights into my first stint at night duty when the former staff started trickling in for former staff weekend.

That was when Nathan R began "acting up."

I really had no clue what I was supposed to do. It was former staff weekend, and I knew this was a bunch who knew all about how to deal with the children, and I barely did.

And I also knew some of these were the group I was originally "supposed to" have worked with, had I came to FMH when it was originally planned.

And...heaven only knew what they were thinking about this tall, awkward guy on night duty.

Things got to a point with Nathan that I had to do something. So...

I eventually decided I had to take him to the CR, which was at the other end of the hall in girls end. Which meant a long walk down the hall, past the dining room and living room. And ALL the formers. I knew they were all staring at us, watching me, criticizing me.

I somehow willed myself to keep walking down the hall toward girls end, with Nathan in tow.

We got to the CR and I unlocked it and we went in and sat down on the mattress that was always in there.

Now what?

I had no idea.

A thought came to me, a thought that almost seemed crazy. It did not fit in at all with what I thought I knew about handicapped children.

Tell him you know what it is like to be a foster and adopted child.

The thought did not catch me by complete surprise. I knew Nathan was someone's foster child, maybe even adopted.

But still...really?

Go ahead, tell him. Do you have a better idea?

I didn't. But this one did not make sense, either.

I we sat there on the mattress, Nathan sitting beside me.

"Nathan, look, I know what it is like."

His eyes got wide.

"I was (this seems so crazy, how is he supposed to understand?) a foster child. I am adopted, too. Do you understand?"

His wide eyes got even wider. "No!"

"Yes, Nathan, I am telling you the truth. I know what it is like to be a foster child and to be adopted. I know what it is like (I have no idea why I am saying this) to not think any one wants you."

A few seconds later, the last thing I expected from him that night happened.

He flung his arms around me and began...

(this is almost unbelievable)

...crying.

We sat there for a while longer and finally it was time that we really had to get out of the CR and go down the long hall past all those formers back to boys end.

We got back to boy's end and Nathan got back in bed and soon fast asleep and I went back to my night duty round of jobs.

Chapter 19

I am not sure what it sounds like for me to say that I did not even know if it was ok to enjoy life.

I was...twenty-two or twenty-three. And barely knew what to do with myself in public. And surrounded by so many shells it is almost amazing that I could walk.

I was almost afraid to enjoy life...actually, I was terrified at the idea that you could enjoy life. I thought life and what fulfillment there was in life came from slavish adherence to a bunch of dos and don'ts.

But eventually I found myself enjoying life a little bit more, and at the same time, feeling extremely guilty for enjoying life...even though I really liked the feeling of enjoying life.

In a way it doesn't really matter what it sounds like.

So, I was surrounded by a bunch that quite obviously enjoyed their lives, at home, and in voluntary service. And I knew that somehow I was supposed to jump the chasm from can't really enjoy life (let alone act as if I enjoyed life) to fully enjoying life.

At one point, I came close...very close, to allowing myself to throw myself into life and actually enjoy life and all the fun and good times that everyone else was enjoying.

Except, I couldn't.

It felt fake, actually.

Well, sort of fake.

I wanted it to be real.

But at the same time I was extremely controlled by what I thought (or knew) my parents back home in Oregon thought.

So, when a day off group of us "had the foolish notion" to rent a red convertible for the day, and I knew my folks would hear about it because a friend from back home saw it first hand and I knew he would inform someone, I emailed mom and confessed to the sin that I had committed.

At least it was declared a sin at the time.

With all of this going on in the background, it is probably not surprising that I had a sort of split mind on all of this "enjoy life" issue. It seems stupid in the extreme to admit it was actually a problem and label it an issue. But it was a huge one.

One day off, we rented a pontoon for the day at Lake Anna. There was a crowd of us...about a dozen.

That evening there was going to be a farewell of sorts for Dennis and his family.

So, we had a fabulously fun day on the lake.

And a lot of fun down at Dogwood pavilion.

And people left and right were telling me they liked how I was "loosening up" and "coming out of my shell".

When I heard that, I was frozen with fear.

And I could not even describe why.

I could not understand why I could not allow myself to enjoy life.

Every Monday evening was Volleyball.

Now, I have never been able to play volleyball very well. Part of this is because I am not really built for sports. Part of this is because back home we were doing good if we played volleyball four times a year.

Add to that, the fact that it was considered "too much" by some in our community to have the one youth meeting a month that we had.

Yes, I know how that sounds. But it is true, probably dumbed down in fact.

So...I was suddenly required to play one game of volleyball minimum every Monday evening. I already knew from the few times I played at Bible School that I was not a good volleyball player. But I was dumped in among a bunch that had lived their lives to play volleyball, and were serious about it...and were incredibly good at it.

And all I knew was, that I wasn't good at it.

So, I would play the required one game, and sometimes more than one, if it was a "good night."

I came to the point of realizing, or believing, that if a particular game began to go really good (at least, good for me), I probably had better quit for a while, maybe for the evening.

I would slip away, make my way down the lane and down the road to the pavilion.

And...stare up at the stars.

Or...come as close as I was able to allowing myself to cry.

Or...make what might sound like strange agreements with God.

Or...fling questions at the stars and the God I hoped was somewhere out among them. Questions like: Why did you allow someone like me to come to a place like this? Why did you allow me, someone who more or less cursed himself into the flames of hell, to even attempt to work at a place like this? Why did you allow me to come here at all, especially since I have almost no confidence or belief in your goodness? Why? WHY? WHY?

It might not be as strange as it seemed at the time that my questions did not get any answers. For the first time in my life I was beginning to be heard by a Father...without being condemned. And it was freeing, and frightening.

Freeing...because I began to suspect that maybe Someone actually had a tiny sliver of respect for me, enough to listen to me, even if He really had no reason to.

Frightening...because I did not know how to tell the difference between a Father's silent listening and silent, but tolerant and perhaps dutiful, disapproval.

So I would swing from silent and sullen, to abrasive and argumentatively assertive...for reasons I could not have placed my finger on.

Especially the one evening in the dining room at the main home when I blurted out, in the presence of the other staff guys who were discussing something (whether or not God actually turned away from Jesus and really forsook Him, or some other related deep subject) "I am not sure that I even believe that God is good."

The walls did not fall. No windows shattered. No one really even seemed surprised.

The only things that began to get cracks in them were my perception of God, myself, and the other staff around me.

It took another late night walk and a painful talk in the cemetery for the light to begin to break in.

And so, I began a habit that carried me through most of the next ten years.

I began a journal.

It was the record of a very confusing journey of faith.

If it can actually be called that; it was a journey, to be sure... maybe the term should be journey into faith. Maybe there is no real difference, and maybe there is.

I almost quit the entire Voluntary Service thing at the end of one year. I had spent nine months as a floater, which was fine as far as that goes. I really did not expect a whole lot more out of myself than that. One after another of the guys who came before and after I did began getting their groups or official positions. One of the guys who came after I did was a brother of someone who had the E boys several years earlier. And it was pretty clear he would have liked to have had his brother's group.

It was not really all that clear that I was supposed to have the group. I grew to the point of liking them, and almost... almost....al..most thinking of them as mine.

People began talking "in the quiet" about the possibility of me getting the E boys group. Some, for totally good reasons, thought it was the worst idea ever to even think of me even thinking about the group.

If I was going to wrap it up at about the end of the year, that would mean giving my three month notice around the first of October.

One classroom and a couple of groups were opening up around the first of October, including the E boys.

I told only a handful of people at the time that I teetered close to putting my three months notice in. Almost everything seemed to scream do it! Hang it up! Go home to who knows what.

So did a phone conversation I was not supposed to overhear.

I was in one of the prayer rooms downstairs in boys staff... trying to read...or pray...or sort out my thoughts.

Suddenly, I heard someone in the other prayer room on the other side of the wall, on the phone...

And what I overheard almost convinced me that I hadn't been wanted here at FMH to begin with, let alone thinking about if I was even fit for one of the groups.

I basically heard my intentions for being at FMH questioned, all but trashed, and that I was pretty much trying to steal a group out from under a guy who deserved the group more than I did. The thing that stung was that most of what he was saying was true.

I wanted to get out of that prayer room, fast. I had gone in there to get some quiet and try to get some clarity of mind... not hear this. But I could not move. I knew that if I moved, the guy on the phone in the other room (who happened to have what you would call clout with the other staff guys and was on the inside with the administration) would hear me and realize he was not as alone as he thought he was.

And what would he would do in response??

His phone call eventually wound down and he went out and hung up the phone.

I could not just sit and stay in the prayer room forever.

Would I be able to look him in the face when we met

As it happened, our paths crossed in the living room.

"Um, I heard you in there."

We exchanged a few words, and suffice it to say that the remainder of the time we were both at FMH there was a sort of cordially tense lets not go there again quiet agreement between us.

So now I was torn between wanting to leave (and go... where? Home, I guess, and to what...how was I supposed to begin to know?)

I could not quite bring myself to go into 304 and tell the administrator that I was resigning in three months...just because I did not see any reason to stay. Just because...a million just becauses came to mind that would not have held any water.

So I agonized...while floating groups. While helping with the various odd jobs I was assigned on extra. While helping with getting one of the houses ready for a staff family to move into. While wondering what on earth was going to happen next.

IF I was asked to take a group, that would mean a six month commitment, at minimum. And I could not imagine, really, anyone on the administration being what would have to be stupid enough to ask me to fill any position. Let alone the E's...given what I had heard and the little I knew about what was being said about me among the other staff.

And, IF I would be asked to take a group, (at this point, the E's were the only ones that the Administration would really have seriously considered asking me to take, and they were, in return, the only ones I would have given a second thought about taking) it would mean that a lot of things I was sure about...were wrong.

I was so sure I would NOT be asked, that when the Administrator called me into his office and asked if I was ok with the C boys, which were coming up before the E boys, would go to the other guy, who had really wanted the E's but also would have liked the C's, I was outwardly like, "Sure. Um, yeh...that sounds good to me."

Inside, I was like "You have got to be kidding me...You are actually going to offer me a group??!!"

I was asked to keep it under my hat for a few days. And I also got a hint that the Administration was considering whether or not to ask me to take the E boys. It was not official...yet.

I gulped, probably blinked in surprise a time or two and said something in reply, then left the office.

About a week or two later, I was still somewhat shocked when my name was called on the intercom to "come or call 304, please."

When I left the office a little bit later, I knew I was going to be the E boys "dad".

I did not know that it would be for almost 16 months.

And I did not know that my mind would be stretched, my endurance would be challenged, or that my heart would be cracked open and almost shattered a number of times in those next months.

My mind would be stretched with a whole world of new facts and a whole new way of looking at and dealing with people. My will to keep on being the "dad" to three, later four, very diverse E boys, would be stretched to the breaking point, and beyond. And my heart would begin to be injected with something it had hardly ever allowed itself to feel or experience or express, and did not know what to do with.

Love, whether human or divine.

Chapter 20

I made a brag that I was not going to be one of those shallow people who went to Bible School and or VS somewhere and landed themselves a boy or girlfriend. And for the most part that was not too hard to live up to. In fact, it was pretty easy to do. If the shallow inclination to want a girl began to raise its head, I wasted no time making sure the thought died of its own. Or I killed it by myself. But of course, I could never, even in my best moments, even begin to imagine why any girl would bother to look at me, let alone waste the time to think about whether or not to say yes or no. So, I assumed it would be an assumed no...therefore, why ask?

And that worked, most of the time.

But there was another piece to the equation, that was seldom discussed.

I knew exactly what mom and dad thought about the whole idea of me and girls...or I was pretty sure I did. I was the second youngest of nine children, and had the chance to see a number of my older siblings reamed out for paying too much attention to girls, or guys as the case may have been. And I knew mom and dad would both say I had way too many issues to even begin to think about girls.

So, by and large I ignored them.

What happens when a kid who was used to being totally controlled in almost every area, used to being regarded too stupid to even make his own decisions, is suddenly and sort of unexpectedly thrust into an environment where you are expected to believe you are an adult? And act as if you are an adult, and eventually, believe that you are an adult.

All that to say...

I was totally unprepared to know how to relate to girls. And at FMH you were pretty much expected to relate well to girls, and everyone. We were all supposed to be a big family.

And I barely knew how to act like that. I barely knew how to relate to other guys. So it was a stretch to expect me to know how to relate to girls.

Oh, and add the everlastingly shameful fact that I have never been able to drive.

It is a wonder I lasted a year at FMH, let alone three and a half years.

With those several strikes against me, I suddenly found myself in the position of senior guy...with a bunch of girls... and no other guys.

And I did not know what I was supposed to do.

I was absolutely ashamed of the fact that I can't drive.

And so, I acted in a very bull headed manner that totally belied how I was really feeling about all this. And I tried to lead out...although I really had no clue how.

The meeting "bombed"...and what reputation I had slid further down the drain, as far as interpersonal relationships went.

What was I supposed to do around a gal who may as well have been a younger sister and seemed so light hearted that I was certain there was not a serious bone in her body (we fought, that is what we did). Or around a gal who was unbearably flighty and...blonde? Or...the list is endless.

The last thing any one would have expected was that I would consider asking any of them out.

And of course, I made a point of fighting and denying any thoughts along those lines, like any good conservative Mennonite boy who wanted to have half a chance of pleasing his authorities and getting a girl (yes, in that order) knew, or had been specifically taught to do.

It is easy to at least act spiritual in the wake of not getting what you wanted...especially if you have been taught it is better. And especially if you have been used to thinking that acting like you have it all under control equals actually having it under control. And especially if your perception of what you have been taught is that perception is more important than reality.

I came to the point of at least appearing like I was too spiritual for...girls.

It would have been commendable, maybe, if it had not been so hollow. The fact that it was more or less successful in keeping girls at bay (among other things)...made it more ironic.

The more spiritual I managed to appear, the more hollow and more inwardly withdrawn I became. In retrospect, it is questionable whether I actually did appear all that "spiritual" after all. And to an extent, more angry and bitter.

There is a deceptive "advantage" to being in service that is sometimes applauded more than it should be. You can shelve, or stuff or ignore your inner, real heart issues while serving. Mostly because you are expected to give of yourself and do the noble thing called "focus on others and not so much on yourself".

You can also convince yourself that you aren't good enough for girls...and that they would not look at you twice if you asked them and a lot of other things. At least I fairly easily convince myself of that.

So it did not make sense when I found myself allowed... almost led...to pay attention to girls. Especially a couple that come to mind that actually caught my eye...but I just knew that I could not...or was not allowed to…or...something.

I had all but vowed that I would leave FMH as single as I was when I got there. And I did, pretty much. And I was pretty much persuaded...to the point of unbelief...that there was no way I could get past it.

I did not believe I was lovable...or want-able...or worth a girl's second thought. And the way I conducted myself around girls more or less insured that was a self fulfilling prophecy.

I developed a reputation that I sort of liked. I was not quite a girl hater...almost, or something. I half way hoped I had a reputation of being a little bit spiritual, as much as saying that makes me laugh...or cry...now.

I was too spiritual...I hoped...to be seen as interested in girls. The only problem is, there was this girl....

The short story is that I just knew I was not really "supposed to" be interested in her. But I was...enough so that I wrote her a letter after she went home after her stint at FMH was over.

Somehow it seems remarkably shallow...stupid...and shortsighted. At the instant I was drafting the letter, I half way knew it was not supposed to be.

But I felt...almost bidden...to ask her anyway.

I also asked God "Why bother asking if it is destined to be a no?"

His answer made sense...sort of.

Ok. That was almost entirely a lie.

It made no sense. That is, if the thought...or answer that I thought I got from God actually was from Him.

Yes, you read that right.

"You need to experience...and find out what it is like to have a girl say no...so you can be a little bit more sympathetic with other guys who get turned down."

Like I said, that word made no sense to me. It might not have even been from God. I knew quite a bit about not feeling wanted in life the way it was. As far as I could tell, it was just the next chapter of the same book.

So I slipped the letter in the mail box one morning when my boys (the E boys) and the Home Ec teacher took our morning walk.

And if my journals of the next couple of weeks are any indication, I experienced what I was convinced was a lot of spiritual growth. I convinced myself that I was focusing more on God and drawing closer to Him.

And perhaps, I was. And perhaps I was trying to prove to God and myself that I was still spiritual. I hoped that maybe if I was turned down, it was because I appeared so spiritual...and not "just" for the thousand and one reasons that I would have listed for turning myself down, if I were a girl and someone like me would ask her out.

So...what I expected happened. I was turned down in a nice enough way, and on the surface became even more "spiritual."

At least, I hoped I looked a little more spiritual.

If I appeared more spiritual, it was a fitting, and perhaps ironic cover up to hide a growing sense of loneliness, self hatred, and subconscious bitterness toward God.

Chapter 21

How are you supposed to act around a group of people who can do everything better than you can? I was around a crowd that could play volleyball "in circles" around me, quite obviously had their act together, and there was a small group that had known each other from Bible School days that were almost best of friends and perhaps unintentionally exclusive. And they could sing...and knew how to sing...and were good at it. And one of the qualifications to being part of this clique was to be able to sing.

Well, I could not sing...not that good anyway. This is not to say I did not wish I could. I wished I could...desperately. I had wished that pretty much all my life. I have wished since I was small that words could flow from my lips. But such has never been the case.

There were some on staff at the time that were jealous of the ones who were asked to join a singing group once it formed. They were jealous because they thought they were at least as good singers as the core group was...and thought they should have deserved to be part of it.

I was jealous...but not really because I was not part of the group. I knew I would never be seriously asked to be in any singing group. I was secretly, or not so secretly jealous of anyone who could sing better than me. And that was pretty much anyone who could sing five notes in a row without flatting.

In typical fashion I got into at least one argument about music and singing and the virtues or vices of a cappella versus instruments...and sometimes the arguments got beyond heated. Especially when I blurted out that I "sort of appreciate contemporary music" and my taste for Rock. This was at a time that I was working among people who at least professed that a cappella was the only music a Christian should listen to. And they were convinced that anything else was practically from hell...at least they sometimes gave that impression, given how guilty they acted when caught listening to instrumental music, or when someone blurted that they could "worship with contemporary music just as well as a cappella church hymnal music."

About this time I was allowing myself to express myself more on paper...in the form of poetry. And I began letting others read some of what I had written...mostly the poetry. As I look back at some of my poems of that time, I am slightly embarrassed at how poor quality they are. But it is where I was at the time.

One afternoon someone more or less attacked me for "showing off" my writing. I was taken aback. In fact...I was taken back to the afternoons back home when I was told more or less the same things. When I was told I was showing off when I wrote. After hearing this person out, I left without saying just a whole lot.

One afternoon, soon thereafter, my answer came to me. So the next time our paths crossed, I said, "I suppose I have as much room to call you down for being proud of your singing as you have room to call me down for being proud of my writing and poetry."

Finding My Voice 153

Our conversations were not without "ripples" before that... but after that, we sort of made sure we gave each other plenty of "berth" at least in that area.

Meanwhile, I was attempting to be "dad" to three, and later, four "E Boys".

There was Danny...who was the picture of insatiable curiosity. And could not stop drooling. And could "talk" in his own brand of sign language. And who loved to throw empty boxes in the incinerator...and pretty much being in the center of everything that was going on.

Then there was Jeremy...who "was not supposed to be able to walk"...yet by the near miracle of patterning had learned to walk...and was almost hopelessly double jointed. His moods swung almost as freely as his long arms and gangly legs... from near euphoria to "dumps" that took days to get up out of. Sometimes he was "flying high" one minute and "crashed" the next. He could not talk...except in what we affectionately called "bop bops".

Then there was William. Who did "nothing" but rock all the time. Who could not tolerate all the noise the other boys made and consequently got into trouble for screaming in anger. Who ran off the first day I floated the group by myself. Who I spent hours holding...trying to figure out. Who "sang" when he was angry...the angrier he was, the louder he sang. Who gave me almost the most grief...but who I grew to love the most of any of the boys.

Since the boys were more or less nonverbal, there were days that I almost did not have to say a word. I picked up enough sign language to be able to "talk" across the room, or down the hall. And not having to talk suited me well for the most part. A lot of the time I did not feel that I had a lot to say. If I did have something to say, I was more comfortable spilling it out in the pages of my journal.

After fifteen months of giving them my best, I began feeling burned out. One morning, as I was giving them their daily showers, I had a moment of honesty and said to myself "I am tired of this...I am tired of these boys."

I needed to get some soap or shampoo or something, so I went down the hall.

When I got back to boys end and continued with their showers, I had a sense of "times up" that I did not want to admit but I knew was true and did not know what I was going to do about it.

It so happened, God had that one figured out before I had time to worry about.

Chapter 22

From the valley of trouble there seems no way out;
My slow feet are heavy, and burdened by doubt.
An enemy stalks me without and within:
My soul is its prey and it seems he will win
The prize that he seeks – it's my soul he'll devour—
Is there no escape from the grasp of his power?
In the depths of this valley a pathway I see:
The path I must follow if I would be free.
Though I creep through this vale at a heart rending pace
The word from my God is a word full of grace.
"A gateway of Hope" at his saving command
Shall arise in the midst of this desolate land.
The enemy's stalking is now turned back in flight;
No longer its prey, I walk on towards the light.
The "gateway of hope" is a foretaste of dawn—
A glimpse of the glory when this vale is gone.
Through the gate I would walk, leave this vale behind
 'Till the fullness of life in the Father I find.
JPB

"He has been diagnosed with what?"
"Something called dementia."
"Um, is that...is that like alzheimers or something?"
"Sort of, but not really."
It was a Sunday evening when I got the call from mom.
Dementia. Something similar to...but different from alzheimers.
I did not know what to ask...or say.
I did know that dad had slowed down some since the tree accident three months before I left for FMH.
I had heard and seen that dad's health, which had been up and down for a while had been getting worse.
"So...um...was it sudden? What caused it?"
"He was just recently diagnosed. As far as the doctors can tell, it may have been going on in the background for...ten, fifteen, twenty years already."
Gulp.
Is there a nice way to say what was going through my heart and mind in the hours and days and months after hearing those words? Probably not.
Especially when I began hearing reports about some of the things dad was doing.

Which was absolutely unlike anything the dad I grew up under was like.

He began to repeat himself. Weirdly. Strangely. One afternoon, I called home to wrap up some bank business which involved taking his name off an account and getting account numbers.

No sooner had I got off the phone than I got another call... from him, this time, telling me something he thought I needed to know (and he had already told me).

It began to sound as if dad actually had a sense of humor.

I never, even on dad's best day, saw so much as a glimpse of a hint that dad had a sense of humor.

I was livid.

He would actually laugh at his own mistakes...serious ones...traffic related ones. That is NOT dad!

He would apparently even laugh in church. Which was a total cardinal sin when I was a youth and teenager.

But when did Dad's mind actually start...literally... unwinding?

Before...before I came around?

Was there something about me, or the other foster children... or the other adopted children that undid him? Was he always... like this and it only now came to the surface?

Or...was it triggered when he was flung out of the tree that terrible morning?

Or was it triggered when he learned that grandpa and grandma did not think as much of him as he thought they had...

Wow...this is getting deep way past my league. But it is a slice of what was going through my mind.

And what did this have to do with me?

It forced me to radically challenge every memory I had growing up at the Bechtels.

Memories that confuse me, even as I drift back in mind to them.

Memories that would be declared false by my siblings.

Memories that the Spirit of God would one night have to validate and powerfully and sadly tell me were absolutely true.

Memories...that have shaped and shattered my perception of myself, what a father is supposed to be like, and what God the Father is actually like.

Memories...of a man I feared...tried desperately to please...but failed to. To the point of frustration...Frustration to the point of intense anger. Anger to the point of hatred. Hatred to the point of..despair. Despair to the point of suicide...almost.

Dad...always extremely serious.

Dad...forever seeming guilty about something he had not done "just right".

Dad...almost never pleased with anything I did. To the point that when he did say he approved of something, it was so far out of character that I refused to believe it.

I really, really did not know how to relate to him. And now, to add to it all the mind numbing fact that he had had this thing called dementia all the time I had called him dad...was devastating.

Which parts of the dad I thought I knew were him for real, and which parts were distorted by the ailment no one knew he had?

The time he discovered I had lied about wiping and hauled me off back to my room and ordered me to lay across the bed with my pants and shorts pulled down as he gave me several whacks with his belt?

Him always taking forever to get ready for church...or anywhere making us late so often, it became an almost whispered joke that "Yeh, the Bechtels are always late."

This was particularly maddening on the two most important nights of the school year: the Christmas and Closing programs. We were rarely ever on time.

Then there were the times that he ordered me to do... ridiculous things. Like cramming a stocking cap on my head before I left for school because, apparently, he thought I needed to wear it.

Or the time I awkwardly...yes, rudely (I was an awkward, self conscious teen) cut in front of one of the preachers after church. Dad made me feel as if it was a sin "almost to death". And I was ordered to confess it to the preacher.

For a long time I didn't. I tried to tell myself how sinful I was because of not being respectful to the preachers, and I laid awake nights...literally...trying at the same instant to convince myself that I did not need to confess any such thing to trying to quell the absolute terror that rose up within me at the thought of having to face the preacher and tell him what dad said I was supposed to.

I finally gathered the courage to say what I knew dad wanted me to say, all the while feeling like it was fake and that I was doing it just to get that off my conscience...if it even mattered or was wrong did not even come close to crossing my mind. I had been told to do it, so I had no choice but to do it, unless I wanted to go to hell. (I practically lived in a suburb of hell, it felt like.)

Ironically, perhaps, dad left me more or less alone. Until I did something wrong. Like the one Saturday when there was so much chaos and turmoil in the house and dad's very presence and manner were simply making it worse (just standing there silently looking at you...in a manner that you knew a rebuke or a long look of disapproval was coming, or...) and I was trying to make a cake or something and instead of getting one ingredient I got another...or else I put something in the wrong container, I don't remember which...

I got throttled.

I don't remember if I actually got hit...but if I did, it would have been a more or less typical Saturday with dad at home.

And the next day, Sunday, I was required, to try to save family face, to play the ultimate hypocrite. At least try to.

Smile and say "God bless you" when it seemed that God was nowhere close by...let alone blessing anyone.

Try to hold appearances together. Pretty hard to do when all week you were forced to live under the tension of a horrid home life (mostly your fault...) and wearing the "school face" so you could survive and maybe keep everyone at school from seeing how tore up you were (seldom worked).

Then Sunday, comes, and your stiff insides (stiff from the tension) insist on beginning to loosen up during church and... announcing their presence with uncalled for, embarrassing rumblings.

That you knew everyone in the auditorium heard.

So...I am not sure which I hated worse...Saturdays or Sundays.

What did I do to get dad...and sometimes mom, so angry at me?

As far as I could tell, the fact that I existed was sin enough... and that I existed in the time and place and manner that I did.

(They were half way convinced I was semi retarded, remember.)

I was totally convinced.

I am not sure if you are supposed to be able to remember your last whipping. I was 19 or 20. It was a Wednesday afternoon and things were in a turmoil. I had done something wrong again (just what, doesn't matter...it seemed I was forever doing something wrong) and so I was hauled off to the back room/freezer room, ordered to bend over the freezer and dad lit in with his belt. Approximately five whacks later I whimpered and shed a few tears, which were followed by several more whacks.

Then we washed up and went out to the patio for supper.

And, I think we went through the motions of going to prayer meeting.

When dad actually tried to show approval or his variety of love...I did not know what to do with it. It was so not like him. I was used to being either ignored, criticized, silently stared at until I blew it, and then...

But...being told he actually thought a topic I had in church was "pretty good"...I had absolutely no context to put it in. I could not even muster the desire to believe that he meant it. It could not be real.

Is it terrible to wonder...if it was his dementia?

But, there is the other, equally terrible question: which one was his dementia?

Or the afternoon of my thirteenth birthday...what was intended to be a father/son outing was a total flop. Sure, it was a surprise. As soon as I got home from school, I heard dad was going to take me "out" somewhere.

I had no idea what I was supposed to think, or do. So, I clammed up and did nothing.

I remember almost nothing about the rest of the afternoon.

That was the last time he attempted something like that. I am not sure if I really ever wanted to do it again. I really never felt free to talk to him...about anything. There were a few times when we would be riding around in the truck somewhere and out of the blue: "Do you want to talk?"

Why would I want to talk, now? I haven't been important enough to bother with talking to up to now. Why would anything be different now?

"Nope."

We would drive on in silence. Me, relieved, and dad...? How was I supposed to know? Maybe he was relieved that I didn't talk much. It was usually worse than messy when I did. I could not say much more than two or three sentences without a painful, awkward pause (which to dad indicated that I was mildly retarded) followed by someone else always finishing my sentences.

So...it became pointless to try to talk much.

At least it seemed to be pointless.

This was the dad who always took what the last conservative preacher said...or what he understood him to say...and ran with it. Or never let you make your own decisions about what books you would buy. Or what music you would buy.

Like the one Sunday I got busted for having and actually listening to an illegal (in our house) tape of a black gospel quartet called Fairfield Four. In an attempt to shame me (I guess) into seeing how devilish it was, dad played it in the stereo in the dining room. I was supposed to feel terrible about listening to such ungodly music.

I felt far from terrible...except terribly angry that I could not make any decisions about what music I liked. Angry...and I was forced to look as if I was sorry, and thus stuffed it all.

All of this formed my childhood and young adulthood. And none of it made any sense.

So...I heard that dad had dementia, which can be likened to the coating on the brain being slowly disintegrated. When a person begins to learn, as a child, a coating of sorts begins to form over the brain, which gets thicker (?) as you grow up and learn.

Dad was gradually "unwinding" or "unlearning"....everything.

A number of my siblings watched this close up, since they lived close by, and it was gradual enough they were able to process it, they said.

I was living in Virginia.

They were all out in Oregon.

I was not able to just sweetly accept this...like the others said they could.

It struck me that everyone was able to handle everything better than I could. Unless they were so used to putting on an appearance of acceptance that they thought it was for real.

During this stage, dad came up with some really far out things, that more or less destroyed a friendship or two, wreaked havoc in general, and caused longtime scars in some of those who got in the way of the words.

One week I accompanied a girl and her boyfriend out to Oregon so they could surprise her parents.

On the way back to the airport, dad, who rode along so he could take the car back, decided then was as good a time as any to let fly about a few "concerns" he had about some things he knew, or thought he knew about how the girls at FMH (Beachys in general....he had an issue with Beachy girls and how "loose" or worldly he thought they were.)

So...he unloaded with an at least ten minute rant that went into how the girls were supposed to conduct themselves, how they should or should not sit on the floor and other things that, really, were neither here nor there nor any of his business.

The poor girl sat there, and to her credit was enabled to hold her tongue through the...tirade.

We drove along in (dad may have thought it was listening to the Spirit's convicting voice) silence. I was seething Why on earth did you have to do that? Now? Why is it any of your business? I hope she is going to be able to forgive you... because I will have a hard, hard time doing it.

The girl meanwhile was seething, as well.

She said later she eventually was able to forgive him. I sure hope so.

It was so close to being in character that I almost think it was deliberate, and not caused by the ravages of dementia.

Unless, of course, him and dementia and his personality and my memories are so intertwined that there is no distinguishing between when he was himself and when he was (for lack of better words) demented.

During one round of night duty, the almost incredible happened.

It was in the middle of a nineteen night stint of night duty. I was folding laundry in the downstairs laundry room. Thinking my own thoughts...if I was thinking at all. It was approximately midnight.

It is time to go look up your real mom.

I wondered if the length of time I was on ND affecting my head.

The next night...same time. Same place. Doing the same thing.

It is time to look up your real mom.

I was almost convinced that I was going crazy. I put it out of my mind, again.

The third night. The same place. Same time. The same words.

It is time to go look up your real mom...

Standing down there in the laundry room, my heart began pounding, hard. My mind began racing. Maybe this was for real.

God had just told me to go look up my real mom.

And that is a story for another time.

Chapter 23

Thy sword has cut away from me
All props, with great severity,
That I had trusted to uphold
Me in my own self – righteous mold.
With violent hand – I thought it so –
You lay my trust in self down low.
Yea, naught remains but wilderness –
Bewildered, shattered, and distressed.
A word dispels the mystery:
"Your wilderness was made by me.
Had you been left thus overgrown,
And your great weakness ne'er been shown,
You never would cry out to me
For strength that I give graciously.
You shall find grace if you but seek
And claim my strength when you are weak."
Ah, grace within the wilderness!
A gift from God, with which to bless
The Israel whom He had cut down:
He builds, and will with grace surround.
God, give me rest, although I must
Be ground, if need be so, to dust.
Thy work is good, your rest will be
My portion while I dwell in Thee.
JPB

The nineteen night stint of night duty finally came to an end. A couple of days later, I decided to call home and break the idea to mom.

I still had my doubts about the whole thing.

Sure, I had called my birth mom and told her that I forgave her. Sure, a few letters and cards had passed between us. Sure, we had even had one or two phone calls.

But...was I really ready to face this woman who...frankly... had totally messed up my life? I had bragged to myself that if we met on the street I would have to be physically restrained from beating her up...or worse.

So...was I really ready?

If this is not a good idea, mom will probably say so right away. If it might be a good idea, I will be able to tell if she sounds even a little bit favorable.

I called out to Oregon.

"I got this sort of strange idea the other night and wanted to bounce it off of you."

"Yes?"

"I think I am supposed to go look up my real mom sometime soon. What do you think of that idea?"

What is she going to say?

Long pause.

I was somewhat unprepared for her reply.

"I have always wanted to meet your family."

We talked for a few more minutes and then hung up the phone.

I sat back in my chair...and experienced that free falling sensation again. That scared yet somehow this is what I am supposed to do feeling.

I was going to go on a flying trip to Oregon. And Pendleton.

And...then the day that is burned forever in my memory... March 19, 2004.

First there was a heart wrenchingly honest talk with R, at D's the evening before. For some reason Dad did not push for me to come home with them after supper at M&S's. I was utterly impressed with R: definitely not "Mennonite" in appearance, but I could not doubt he and L really wanted to be Christians.

I wish I could always be as honest as I was at D's and in R's van. I am so glad that God told R to take me over. We NEEDED that brutal, brotherly honest talk. Especially about when he left home in response to mom's 24 hour ultimatum that basically left me sit in the dust of his escape. (I thank you, Abba, that all the toughness, impossibilities of life, the sins and all that may come to memory MUST come through the door that reminds the bringer and the rememberer that ALL , under God, is forgiven!!)

How are you supposed to describe a conversation with people who more or less watched you grow up, and observed, maybe from a distance, your life at its worse? Maybe one day I can be fully free to be bluntly honest —— I was taken a number of steps closer to that today. And I am thankful for being able to clear my soul and mind with the folks en route to Pendleton.

We pulled into Pendleton about 12:40 pm and wound up at a KFC at the SW side of town. The folks went in and I went over a block, then over the street to a gas station for a phone and called my mom, informing her of our whereabouts.

I literally could not eat. For some reason, I subconsciously knew I had memories of that very KFC...and apparently, they were painful ones.

Then we went to Aunt Kathy's place where Grandma Sutter and an uncle were waiting. It was an indescribable combination of not having seen anyone of my family: yet immediately feeling at home and as if I belonged with them. I felt like I had come back to seal off the childhood chapter of my life. I felt lost, dazed, not quite remembering yet fully...I almost comprehended what I was doing...sitting there, talking with my aunt, uncle and grandma.

I was...shocked...when I heard Aunt Kathy say "I always knew you would come back. I just knew you would." Numb... that might be a better word to describe me. (If I was numb, maybe I am feeling an exquisite form of pain in the wake of it all). The healing began that up till then had not been fully allowed to.

I can still feel the confusion and frustration at the phone booth; one apparently dead; the other one clicked and my call went through. (This was a couple of years before I had a cell phone.)

Is there a way to describe the strange feeling of having once been in Aunt Kathy's house? I took one last long, lingering gaze in the living room, with the couches and fireplace on opposite sides. I took in the kitchen with the vaguely familiar small sinks, counters and dark paneling. The dining room with the painting above the stove. The small old stands. I could ALMOST close my eyes and remember.

Remember when I used to play in this very living room... tear around in this very house...

I handed Grandma A, K, and D (each separately) a plaque with a poem I wrote on it.

There is something I could not comprehend. Dad insisted on telling Aunt K who wrote it. (This is probably just another thing I have to put on the list called "dad had dementia, and was not entirely responsible for what he did".) Aunt Kathy appreciated it any way, and put it on a top shelf of the hutch in the dining room right by the kitchen.

I got dad and mom's actual affirmation that I have what it takes to be a man in my own right. This kept me on an even keel...sort of...

The phone rang twice during my final talk with Aunt K ("Oh, it's HER...we will just let it ring")

Then, finally...and in some ways, still too soon...we made our way to where my mom lived.

"111 S. E. 6th" scrawled over the basement entry door.

She was standing on the sidewalk waiting for us.

Striking red hair and puzzling eyes round lensed glasses (she said she liked mine better)

Admission and evidence of depression (she said she's on disability because of it and cannot work)

I instinctively knew I had to do part of this...alone. Perhaps I was still rattled by how dad had messed things up, and created a sort of awkward situation at Aunt Kathy's. Any way, mom and dad asked if I wanted them to come down with me.

I said I wanted to go down myself.

They had not been in my life when I still lived in Pendleton, and I sensed instinctively that I could not connect in the way we needed if I was under their...would it be criticizing, disapproving, stiflingly controlling...gaze?

I had 15-25 minutes alone with my mother before the folks came down. She told me her dreams of becoming a writer; how she played violin as a child ("we were all expert at it...do you play any instrument?") She rattled off her disappointment that she never really was able to learn to play an instrument.

She asked what was in the bag I was holding.

I told her it was something for her.

She asked again, "What's in the bag?"
"Open it and see."
"I am scared to."
"Then I will open and give it to you."
She read over it, half murmuring, half what was it, weeping? When she realized I had written it, her response was beautiful.

She said inside of five minutes that she liked me, and I returned the same with an arm around her shoulder.

"I am proud of your writing...it's what I always wanted to do...keep it up; have you gotten it published? have you thought of it?

She told me her version of the REAL story about my birth and how she and my dad hitchhiked from Pendleton to MI in the heat of summer, then were forced out of the house they were in. "They said, 'you'll just have to leave".Terry will stay here.' So we both left." I heard about their hitchhike BACK to Pendleton while she was pregnant with me.

It was a much more human, and sad story than I had dreamed. I cannot count the number of times I embraced her today. The folks came in and chatted about this and that. She looked over my writings that I had along somewhatâ€¦then suggested prayer.

I will never know if dad felt I took the limelight away from him or not. I initiated it and led out. Part of me did not really know if I cared or not. It was, after all, my mom, and I was not really willing to be hindered in what I wanted to do by his awkward, and frankly, disconnected attempts to control.

Especially since he had just claimed that he thought I had what it took to be a man in my own right.

"Do you want to pray?"

"I don't know how. So she "just" talked to God and it moved me deeply.

Then dad closed.

Of course, we had to take pictures.

"I promise I will write and stay in contact."

Much more went on in that basement apartment, but it will stay in memory.

After final words at K's, we checked in at our motel and got a bit of rest. Then we headed up to Minthorn Lane, with dear old Millie up ahead, leading the way. Going back that gravel lane on the Reservation was like driving into memory city. We were there after dark; it was a new trailer, but approx. the same position as the one I recall from 4 years old. I still remembered the trailer across the field...even took pains to look and see that YES it was still there.

Memories galore. We talked about my first day in the Bliss' house as a "big for my age" 3 year old.

"I thought," said Millie, "I'd never be able to keep up with him!"

We talked about Head Startâ, confirming what I have always thought: I was reading at age four. Millie retold how I "blew away" the man's mind at Hawthorne Elementary with the battery of tests.

"Can he spell his name?" (I did)

"Can he...can he read?"

"Give him a book." So they gave me a book, and "You, with a grin from ear to ear read it right off."

"Well...if he can count, he can spell, if he can read, he can come!"

Then there were of course one or two mildly embarrassing stories to tell about me.

"He always had a mind of his own."

"Mmmmm I (gag) like (gag) Brussels sprouts!?"-when asked to eat "just a little of it". "I don't WANT to go to bed!!"

School being the next day, I went, dragging my feet and crying to bed. "Do you want me to give you a spanking?" "NOOOOOOOOOO!!!!"

Tea and ginger bread. I was honored to serve the tea to the folks.

McKay School and the church..Memories...many more came back in days to come.

"Their Mattie" an amazing autistic boy who was born blind (they thought) and yet sees with help of strong glasses, an absolute perfectionist with a rollicking, dry sense of humor. Bliss' "third Peppie" except that this dachshund is a female ;).

I felt like I had finally came home!

Then pictures with the folks, with Bliss'. "It's niney" (9 pm).

Save this, my soul, for when the memories do fully come; and then read "the last chapter of the book."

Going to Bliss' was the dessert on a very difficult, but strengthening "meal" of a day. Thank you, Abba, for impressing it on me to do this trek into the land of my childhood. No questions asked verbally; but many answers gotten to a lot of my heart questionings...the healing of finally beginning to find where I belong.

A new day has dawned. Thank you Abba. Amen.

We spent that night at the Travelodge in Pendleton. I wrote several pages about that day in that room...late into the night.

The next day, Saturday, we left the Travelodge...after having to go back when I realized that I had forgotten my camera in my room.

Once back home, after the five hour trek from Portland to Estacada, mom came out to the porch where I was sitting, in a daze.

"So, what are you thinking about it all?"

I was still in sort of a shell shock. And I didn't know what I thought. Or how I felt. I was more or less numb.

"I don't...I don't know. There are really no words for it."

I didn't have "words for it" for a long time.

Because it was just the beginning. Of what, I really had no idea.

The week after I met my biological mom was sort of an emotional mine field. How was I supposed to put into words the...trauma...the questions...the thousand and one conflicting thoughts and feelings that began to surface after that first meeting?

I wish I could say that I had a long heart to heart with mom and dad after we got back to their place. But we didn't. I could not think of the right words for what was going on in me.

How was I supposed to process everything?

Even now I am not sure that I have sorted everything out.

I hope that is okay.

Maybe a lot of things that strike me as not okay are okay after all.

Someone is not going to be really cool with what you just said.

Oh, will you just shut up?

Midway through the following week I flew back to Virginia and Faith Mission. I spent a bit of time on the flight back pondering some pros and cons of what had just gone on.

Pros: I had finally made the step of meeting my mom.

I had what turned out to be the last real talk with dad and mom.

This takes me, almost without wanting to, to the cons...

It was the first time I saw my adoptive dad with the effects of dementia.

The effects of the dementia were subtly apparent in ways that I didn't understand. This includes him saying things to me that, to this day, I am not sure whether or not he actually meant. I am pretty sure that I am not at liberty to repeat some of what he said. It stung...hurt, actually. Deeply. Terribly. It left what became an almost life defining wound in my spirit. And, I do not pretend to have gotten "past it."

We as a family had known for a while that dad was diagnosed with dementia. And the family back home in Oregon had "front row seats" as dad began his decline. It didn't help that I was all the way in Virginia and saw and heard only from a distance.

I got back to Virginia sometime during the middle of the week and by Saturday I had my mind made up about something. I would hand in my three month notice.

Maybe it was premature. Maybe. I may have overstayed my welcome at FMH, actually (I had been there three and almost a half years at that point). Maybe it was ill advised, but I decided it was time to move on to a place I knew very little about, but had visited once with a friend a couple of summers prior, out in Indiana.

A place called Fresh Start.

In my final months at Faith Mission, I managed to almost destroy several relationships and make a few enemies for myself. I discovered that I was still a raging bundle of nerves that literally exploded given the chance.

Chapter 24

Several days after I left Faith Mission, I filled out an application for service at Fresh Start.

A day or so later, I got news that Grandma Brothers had passed away, out in Oregon.

So I got a flight out to Portland from Indianapolis and was out in Estacada for a couple of weeks. I think I made a bus trip to Eastern Oregon and looked up my mom and family on her side. I also dropped in on the Blisses.

It was finally the morning to get on a plane and head back to the Midwest. As I was waiting for one of my brothers who would take me into the air port, I was chatting with another, older brother.

We discussed my seemingly spur of the moment decision to head off to Fresh Start. One of the last things he said, in parting, was, "You do know where this direction might take you, don't you?"

The next several years would show whether or not he was right.

I returned to Illinois and made arrangements to go over to Fresh Start for the required interview.

I went, sure of a couple of things. God had done a work in my life and It would be obvious to anyone who was spiritual enough to see it.

My friend and I were at Fresh Start for the weekend. My appearance and how I carried myself were awkward enough that nothing indicated God has done a work in this man's life.

We arrived on a Friday evening. The interview was scheduled for Saturday forenoon. We slept in what they called the dark room.

I survived the staff interview Saturday morning, somehow. We finished up just before brunch. After brunch they were going to help one of the staff families move...someone named Virlin Yoder, who was shop foreman at the time.

We helped them move.

As we were standing around talking, Michelle, the administrator's wife, began asking who I was and where I came from. We discovered that our families knew each other quite well. Our parents had been best friends at one point...they had even lived in my home community, Estacada, Oregon, for a while.

I don't remember very much about the rest of that day. We went to church Sunday and I got my introduction to one of Fresh Start Chapel's traditions. The visitors "get to" stand and be introduced.

So my friend introduced me, mentioning that I was "spying out the land".

That was sometime toward the end of July of 2004. By the middle of August, I was at Fresh Start. Before I left the auditorium that morning, I informed Tim that I had pretty much decided I would come.

A huge part of me went to Fresh Start to prove to myself that I could do something. I hoped in some way to prove that I was...spiritual. My efforts failed right off the bat. I proved my fear of man and total insecurity and desperate need for approval. I had no idea how to go about "counseling". I was the "dumb one" in my own eyes, swinging between not saying anything and getting called down for being "closed" to saying too much, too forcefully and passionately.

It began the Saturday evening I arrived and moved my things into Fresh Start. The staff and guys were away helping another family move when I got there. My friend who brought me over from Illinois helped me haul my things in and then bade me farewell and left me to figure out what I was going to do next.

I put away some of my things and then took a walk into town and bought my first cell phone.

That evening after supper, one of the houseparents was showing me how to run one of the clothes washers. He made a comment that I interpreted as meaning you are really stupid, right?

I began to wonder why I had come.

The next morning in church, during introduction period, something happened that I was sure proved that I was stupid.

Virlin was moderating after Sunday School. I thought he said something about introducing all the staff. So after I introduced myself, instead of handing the mic back to the usher who had brought it to me, I handed it off to the staff guy next to me.

This resulted in a remark from Virlin about there being some misunderstanding. So I quickly realized my mistake and tried to put it out of my mind. But the embarrassment had already begun to work.

I was certain these people thought I was stupid and that the only reason they let me in as a "counselor" was that they needed staff badly enough to let in anyone who came waving an application.

It was clear to me that I could never be as well spoken as most of the staff guys were. I hadn't had half the experience or done a fraction of the reading some of them had. I almost believed I had been mistaken about what I thought God had done in my life. I knew that I could never be good enough to be a counselor.

What had persuaded me to come to Fresh Start in the first place?

Fittingly, I had no clients at first, which was probably more of a mercy than I knew.

One Wednesday afternoon, I opened myself up for staff sociogram. This is an exercise where others in the group point out "blind spots" and attempt to help you work through them.

I completely failed that first staff sociogram. I felt suddenly blindsided and did not "graciously" and "maturely" accept it.

I took the material to heart, which was apparently the wrong thing to do. I was actually driven to tears as I saw the state of my spirit and heart. Which did not seem to be the intended or acceptable response?

I actually had the weakness of character to cry.

I was brokenhearted. And my ability to be a counselor was called into question.

This shadowed me the entire time I was at Fresh Start.

When we had a staff sociogram again, my response was not a whole lot better. I again took it entirely too much to heart. I allowed it to "crush" me.

The third time we had a staff sociogram, I was desperate... and livid. I decided to clamp on an iron face and showed little or no response to the material that was given to me.

And, perhaps incredibly, I was lauded for having matured so much.

Did I mention that I was livid inside?

This convinced me that the whole thing was, in fact, just a game.

My final staff sociogram seemed like little more than a game of trivial pursuit. I reviewed the list of "blind spots," sins of character if you will, and inwardly thought, is that all the better you can do? I hardened my soul and spirit over that time because it seemed that is how you got through the game.

Chapter 25

I mentioned that I did two terms at Fresh Start. One was an actual, official term that lasted three and a half years. It proceeded pretty much the way it began. I eventually was allowed to attempt to be a counselor.

If results are an indication, I failed as a counselor as well. I had six clients, ranging from ex convicts to Amish. Some of them were declared "honorable complete" when they left. At least one left because he couldn't "stand the love". Those were his exact words.

As far as I know, most of them soon went back to their old lives.

I got word one July morning that my biological mom had been found dead in her apartment in Pendleton. She had died of natural causes, as far as any one knows. It was a combination of the heat of summer and her poor health.

Her remains were cremated and I am not exactly sure what became of them. For a while they were in an urn on a back shelf in my grandparents place. In the following several years, both grandparents passed away.

I really do not know what became of my mom's remains.

The only thing I do know is that God had timed perfectly when to tell me to go meet her.

I say briefly, and I say this respectfully, because my mom had mental and physical problems of her own. Our conversations were good, as far as they went. But there was too much evidence of the state of her mind to ignore.

Our interaction, which included phone and letters sometimes swung from words of deep love and affection, from her, to words of near hate and regret that she had brought me into the world.

I did not really know how to process all of this.

My oldest adoptive sister also passed away during my first term at Fresh Start.

The afternoon that I met my mom for the first time, she gave me my dad's phone number, saying that she would love it if I called my dad. I had way too much to process already with meeting her, so I put it off.

I had off and on contact with my mom's sister Kathy, so I decided to write her and see if she knew anything about my dad's whereabouts.

She wrote back, and included a phone number and address that she thought maybe were his.

So, I had his phone number and I had what was supposed to be his address. The only thing I didn't know, was...was he still alive? And, if he was, I had no idea if he would want to meet me. He left during my early child hood and was gone without a trace. My mom had told me, and Aunt Kathy verified this later, my dad was in "poor health". I did not even know if he was still alive.

I had two options, neither of them were easy. I could call the number Aunt Kathy had given me and risk whatever would happen. Or I could write a letter and risk not getting a reply or any of several things.

There was a third option, which on the surface would have been easier. But I had gotten into this thing too far to be able to back out of it now.

I wrote a letter to this man who was supposed to be my dad...and who I had no conscious memory of...and that I didn't even know if he was still alive.

Wednesday afternoon, I saw a letter in my mail box.

My knees suddenly went weak.

I reached in to the mail box and gasped.

It was from HIM!

Here is an email I wrote soon after, that goes into some detail.

Good evening to you all.

I am not sure what I am supposed to say, so I will begin with the first thing that comes to mind. It has been an interesting, somewhat intense time around here lately. There are lots of changes going on here at FS...some good, few comfortable.

For some time I have been pondering the idea of looking up my natural father. (It would have been the wishes of my mom that I do this long ago, soon after I finally met her. She actually gave me his address, phone number at the time. I was not ready for that step at the time. So I have delayed and not done it and doubted that it was the time.Untill recently.) On the eighth, I drafted and sent off a letter of inquiry to this man who was my dad. I have no recollection of him from childhood. I have only one picture of him and my mom while they were together, which lasted a few years. My parents never were married to each other. I have since found out my dad is married, and has been for a number of years But I am running ahead of myself.

I sent the letter hardly knowing what to expect...if he was alive, still. Would he even want to contact me, this little tyke he had not seen for 28 years? If he did reply...what kind of a letter would it be? On the 17th I got a reply. It was put face down at FS in my mail box, and I was almost sure it was a return to sender...it was the exact same as the envelope I had sent it in. Behold, it was a reply. From HIM!! I almost could not open it, at first. I went up to my office and opened it alone.-(I sort of have a habit of things like that. I was alone in my mom's apt for 20 or so minutes when I first re met. There is sort of a "felt need" to have to do some scary things of that sort alone. The contents of the letter literally blew me away. More or less acknowledging his wrong in the past and (I thought commendably) refusing to make any excuses. He wrote that the only thing he could do is ask for my forgiveness for not taking responsibility and so on. I learned a few painful details about his side of the story over the time I was officially put up for adoption. (I was 1 and a half or so.)

I read his letter several times before the reality began sinking in. I cannot explain the roller coaster of thoughts and emotions that swept through me the next several days. (Note to self: and you thought you had come a long ways in the area of forgiveness..?)

I had providentially requested this weekend off. At the time, I knew not what for. I knew I had to make a phone call...and I was almost scared spitless at the idea.

Thursday evening there was an anti drug rally at the Simon J Graber complex. (This is not a digression, although it sounds like it.) Among the speakers was this lady who gave her testimony. Absolutely incredible. She had gone and done pretty much all there is to do in the drug, etc scene. The thought hit me HARD that this sounded somewhat like something my bio. mom would have/ could have said...at least in regard to how low down she was.

This...while trying to decide if, when and how to respond back to my dad's fairly obvious desire for me to respond. It was so obvious, he gave me his phone number.

Late Friday afternoon rolled around. I had done almost every thing else I could do to keep my mind of the impending call. Finally, God gave me the courage to push send on my cell phone. I got an answering machine with HIS voice. I gulped and could not do it to leave a message.

Several minutes later I called again and the owner of the voice on the machine answered on the first ring. After finally realizing who each other were, we TALKED...for about forty minutes. I still can almost not comprehend that I did it. Those minutes helped begin put some pieces in the puzzle regarding who I am, etc. In brief, he was a Vietnam vet, a life long alcoholic. By his own admission, he believes in God, "in my own human way." I had heard that he is a laid back, quiet sort of man,...and judging from one conversation, fairly plainspoken. One of the first things I did was to assure him that by the grace of God, I forgave him, and do not hold what he did to his account. (Talk about a breathtaking act of God there, now.)

There is a lot I could say, but this is getting quite too long. Before I hung up, (we were both sort of reluctant to) I reiterated my forgiveness twice, told him I loved him, and actually called him dad!!!!

I am still blowed away at it all.

Grace is actually pretty incredible,

jpb

Here are some of my journal entries from around this time. They tell the story better than any attempt to reconstruct it would be able to.

4/26/07

God,
You alone can hear,
And understand, the mumbled rumblings
Of my wondering heart.
I stand confused...yet forced to paste
Upon my wondering brow
A trustful face.
I have no way to put in words
What I don't understand
Since days ago I made a call
And first spoke to the man
That all the records show
Is the one that I should call
My dad.
No picture, God, have I in mind,
of who my father is....
No voice...no touch...not one faint memory.
The only clue I have to guess
Is a little faded picture of
My mom and dad and me.
What do I feel...? I do not really know.
What I thought was just abandonment
Was not an easy letting go.
He said my good was on their minds
Although little I perceived it.
In spite of widely wandering ways,

They said they hoped and prayed the best for me....
Long I failed to believe it.
I'm twenty nine, and all the time
He was a faceless name to me.
I feared...I know not what I feared...
But he had waited years for me.

4/27/07

I do not yet begin to know
How I'm supposed to process this.
It seems the picture I'd construed
Was simply wrong. Amiss.
Ah, how to lay aside the lies,
Although there were some truths.
The truths themselves are fairly easy to relate;
It's the lies that appall me.
It seems the picture I clung to
Included aspects I have found
Are not correct at all.
Yet some are true...this mix
Of truth and lie confounds me.
How can I know the truth, the lie
When they are so closely entwined
In memory and what is starting to appear
A baseless fantasy?

4/28/07

I got a letter from him in the mail today.
An eight line note, and three undated
Photographs.

I glanced at the handwriting and wondered
Was he sober when he wrote this?
I assume he was, at least, the day I called.
Three pictures of a bearded, graying man.
The man is the same as in the picture from
When I was just a tyke in Seventy seven.
The same...yet decades older, obviously.
I am contemplating what to send in my letter
When I respond to him...
Some pieces I have penned; some poetry?
I guess I may as well let him see that side of me.
This makes me wonder what they will be sending
(my grandparents) of mementos of my father's
younger life.
I know one thing that I will send;
A photograph of me that was taken recently.
Favor for favor, I suppose. He sent me some of him.
I wonder: Will he really want to meet me; once he gets a pic
Showing him what I really am?
And then it hits me square: That is probably one of the things he wondered
When he mailed me these pics of him.

4/29/07

I got a phone call from him again this evening
On the way back from the singing at Canaan Church.
The service there was a blessing, although nothing could have prepared
Me for the moment and conditions when I got the call.
I actually let voice mail get it. There was too much music, talking going on,

I am not sure that there was not any fear of man; of what the other guys would think
If they heard me call and talk to him and call him dad.
He wondered if I had got the pictures and he said they are getting some other things around to send me.
After an hour of indecision, I finally returned the call and talked to him,
In the van surrounded by the fellows in the van, after all.
I'm not sure what I am scared of, or if it is really fear.
I am just at loose ends about it all, is all I know to say.
I found out that Darlene (his wife - would have been my step mom) was gone for the weekend,
Also at a church function. Something about song leading or ministring for the deaf.
A bit of an exchange about the long fingers "that he gave me" and comments about piano playing
Livened up the conversation quite a bit.
So now I need to be collecting artifacts to send his way. God knows I am not sure what to send
That would represent what has gone on these 28 years.

4/30/07

So, is there a word
For how you feel
When God destroyes
The lies you lived upon
And gives a glimpse
Of what is real?
9:50 am
Had a chat with JS just a few minuites ago.
Confessed that I am weary of being "a mentor, etc..."

Have way too much to try to figure out.
Need to leave this place of absolute activity and get some solitude.
Even if it kills what is left of the rest of this people pleasing shell
That remains on parts of me.

5/1/07

Not sure what I got done today that was of any real use.
What I mean by use, I am not really sure.
Trekked out to Hardees and took the goods to the park and
Enjoyed a leisurely lunch out on one of the covered swings there.
Read a substantial bit in LOTR. For a "bad" book, that tome is one that is screaming
Something to me through the story line. I know what it is, and yet I don't.
I am hard pressed to know why the character Aragon so calls to me. I can see little resemblance
Between him and myself...and yet, if I am honest, yes I can.
More than I have honesty or bravado to relate.
I made myself write for an hour on that writing project I am in the middle of.
Studied Grace with the help of a Herbert Lockyer volume on all the doctrines of the Bible.
Oh, yah. I did get my paycheck deposited at the bank
And got most of the music of a song somewhat down pat.
This evening, allowed myself to wonder what real life will be like...away from FMH or FS.
I pondered again how much of my VS experience was to "prove I am someone."

God reminded me of the time while I was still back home, just starting to think about VS. I was reminded

That God seemed to ask me "What if I ask you to be in service for 5 years?"

It has been over five...

The only prospects I have now is to wander out into some form of wilderness and

(Contrary to my makeup or what I mistake for common sense)

Go aside and rest.

5/29/07

This is written on a Tuesday about the weekend just past.

Me and HJP were up to McConnellsville, OH for an FMH reunion, for the 2002 group.

Most of the group made a no show. There were about 20 people there, all told.

Sat. afternoon, just before hopping on the Vball court, my cell phone rings.

It is my natural father. (Cell phone service is not very good in those hills of OH.)

He asked how I am and what I am doing. I told him in brief.

He said that he wanted to tell me he got the pic I sent. "You are a good looking young man."

Wow.

He said that grandpa on his side was not doing to well, health wise.

Sunday eve, on the way down from OH my phone rings again. It is my Aunt...my dad's sister, in NC.

Supposed to be sending me some info and geneology stuff. A teaser: the family tree has been traced back to the 1400s.

Waiting......

9/14/07

It has been a long time since I heard a word from him.
I emailed my second cousin Jessica a month ago regarding any genealogy stuff she may have. I have not heard a peep from her. I did send her my new email address. I guess eventually I should get her my new address here in Arcola. Part of me likes the town; part of me hates it; the sane part of me attempts to weigh in and remind me that I am really quite worn out from VS and right now is not the time to try to determine whether I like, love or hate my new town.

In October, I plan on taking the train out to Oregon. I haven't been out there or seen family for over a year. I also want to return to Pendleton and possibly make my way to Walla Walla.

Only you know, Abba, if you will give me the courage to actually follow through on my plans to look my father up. Also, you only know if I will ever have the brass to make reconnections with Jensen's. Part of me wants to... A lot of me is totally scared of the idea.

(This is taken from a combination of journal entries and memory.)

10-22-07 Portland-Hood River-The Dalles-Stanfield-Pendleton

Mom took me in to Greyhound in the morning. The bus was due to leave around 11:30 am. We left around noon. I had an empty seat beside me until Stanfield. Made some use of the semi solitude and read some in the Word. Read the first chapter of Philippians. Verse 6 "...He which hath begun... will perform it until the day of Jesus Christ."

This was a great confirmation and promise for the intended plans of the week ahead, as it turned out.

I had a number of things I hoped would happen. It was my first time back in Pendleton since my biological mom and grandma passed away (2005, 2006, respectively). I wanted to see where my life all began and sort of get a feel of the world of my early childhood. I doubted it would help make much sense of all the events of yesteryear, some I remembered vividly, and others I have been told just recently. I wanted to reconnect with my aunt as well. And take a few pictures... something I had not accomplished very well in past visits.

I hoped it could be arranged to meet my dad on this trip. I decided that even if there was no meeting, just getting my feet on the streets of Pendleton and seeing what there was to see would make the week a success.

The bus rolled in to Pendleton forty minutes late. Millie Bliss was waiting at the stop. (The Bliss' were my foster parents from age 3-6.)

I quote from my journal of the 23rd.

"*Huge afternoon. I walked almost end to end in Pendleton. Surprised Aunt Kathy by showing up at their front door (11 a.m.). I was almost ready to leave, etc, when I glanced up the side walk and saw someone coming up the street...it was her! I had been trying to call; but she has a policy of not answering "strange" phone numbers. She saw the "Indiana #" and "wondered". As she approached her house, I could see her mouth the words, "Is that Josh?!" We had a good chat (over an hour)*. *Conversation ranged from my early child hood to a rehash of my mom's situation to her and my dad's relationship to her "aggressor" his passive, easy going response to her basically attempting to provoke fights and arguments. Such as one time Grandpa and my dad were playing chess at Grandpa's. Apparently for no reason, my mom flared up and threw a cup of scalding hot coffee at my dad. It appears (as per my aunt) that my mom didn't really want any of the help or opportunities offered to her to improve her lot, behavior, and lifestyle. (Today it would be diagnosed as Bipolar.) She reportedly hung out with various "characters"—mostly of ill repute; at least one was an ex-con (the one that called the police after he found her passed away in bed in her apartment). I guess I will find out tomorrow what kind of man my father is. We talked some about Grandma's passing and grandpa's condition. (He seems to have been something of a packrat, from what I can gather… I was in their living room…I can understand why they talk about "Sutter's clutter"… that may be an arch understatement. Aunt Kathy and I also talked about my mom – as of yet her remains are out in the "doll shed" [Grandma made and collected dolls, as well as collecting and selling antiques.] out back behind Grandpa S.' house, in some sort of urn. It appears that the family is still in some sort of shock. My mom and then Grandma passed on within seven months of each other…quite unexpected; although hindsight makes one fully aware of signs that were inadvertently ignored. So… the visit with Aunt Kathy was a sobering mix of sad and glad.*

[The following paragraph took place between about 12:30 pm and 2:30 pm]

I went sort of the long way around to grandpa's house from A. Kathy's. I went down to S. E. 6th and got a picture of the building where my mom lived at the time of our very memorable first meeting...also the apartment where she passed away. (Kathy also said apparently the place was broken into between the times of her death and being found...the apartment was in shambles. Other possibilities do come to mind.) Then I crossed Court Street and made my way to grandpas; by way of Emigrant St, by CSD. (Having the background music that plays during an ominous or depressing scene in some stories or movies may have been in order as I rounded the corner.) Over grown. Run down. (The house grandpa lives in [he is 77 years old] is over 100 years old.) Amazingly, A. Kathy said, she found the deed to the house. (I refuse to try to describe the inside of the house. Photos sort of do justice to the outside...I hesitate to ask leave to take pictures of the inside. I may leave it to memory and imagination. (This is getting LONG!!!) I could say a lot about my impressions of the place. Forgotten and worn out and on the "back side" of the bridge/viaduct. I had had sort of a sense of coming from the poor end of town. My suspicions have been very much confirmed. It was pointed out where I was born...and lived, at least for a short time. It was a top story apartment in a building that has since been demolished. Also the little cottage of a house (also close by) seems to have been removed when the new interstate came through. I had vague memories of going up the street a couple blocks to "Charlie's"; a bit of a store. The store building is still there, after all these years. It is now a Bahai'i fellowship center. I also made my way back to CSD. I asked if they could let me see my childhood records. For various reasons, under existing adoption laws, they could not unseal "sealed" records.

So, I went down Emigrant Street, passed Hawthorn School. (I went there in Head Start.) I had quite a few memories there. I went a ways down the street and had lunch at KFC. I suppose the restaurant was there when I was young. It was where we stopped for lunch the first time the folks and I came over to Pendleton to meet my mom. (They ate; I couldn't have eaten a bite at the time.) That KFC has a lot of memories... some likely buried. I then made my way up toward Aunt Kathy's block on Court Street.

Around 2:30 I showed up again at grandpas. This time I went in. Aunt Kathy had taken lunch over and told Grandpa and my uncle I was coming. They were expecting me. I hung around and made small talk. It was sort of awkward. (This uncle is sort of a long, mysterious story, so is grandpa, for that matter.)

I went down to a bit of an espresso stand and got a cappuccino. Millie picked me up around three that afternoon. From where I waited, at the U haul parking lot across from the Bahai'i center, you can see both Aunt Kathy's and Grandpa's. The viaduct is directly behind the U haul property and between Kathy's and grandpas.

I guess it reveals to me how very small my little (rather mixed up) childhood world was..."

Oct 24th was the day. I anticipated and dreaded it both.

I quote from my journal of the 25th. "Now that it is a day since the events of yesterday, maybe I am clear minded enough to chronicle yesterday's events.

Millie took me down to the Pendleton Library, where I got online and did some genealogy, name research stuff. This was after I realized I knew nothing of my ancestors' names by memory. After about an hour and it was getting around lunch time, I took off down the street to DQ.

My dad had said we would meet around 3:30pm. They have an hour to drive down from Walla Walla, Washington. So I somewhat nervously ate my lunch. On the way back, I stopped at a small Christian book store to get a small gift for my dad and his present wife. On the way back to the Till Taylor Park (where we would meet), I called up a friend and told him what was about to transpire.

Two and three o'clock sort of passed in a blur. I suppose I looked a sight. Pacing back and forth along the iron fence around the pool… finally walking around the block via St. Mary's Church and around by the main road and up in front of CSD and over to the park again. As I was about to cross the street back to the park, I saw a van pull up and park. A sixth sense told me it was them. I think she got out first, and then he got out. (A giant of a man) A self described, un - apologizing long haired bearded hippie coming back to the park and the block and the area where a lot of stuff happened. The fact that he is a Viet Nam vet, and had for sometime studied for nursing, added a lot of intrigue. These things set in motion a sometimes mystifying series of events that had led to where we all were today. My dad is a combo of soft spoken, gruff voiced, hippie, yet polite; extremely likeable, and very much NOT afraid to say exactly what he thinks. He mentioned that coming down to Pendleton opened up a whole bunch of memories about how rotten life was back then…the foolish decisions they made… their literally dumpy lifestyle, etc. We made sort of a point to not dwell on the things of "back then." He said that he told D. (his present wife) "this is a shitty situation." "Why?" she asked. "This situation was supposed to be closed…over." [This conversation had been en route to Pendleton.] One we had been visiting and learned to know each other a bit; he said "this has been the best day of my life." He said that he was proud to see what I have made of my life. (He said he liked what he saw...in words that I hold to be a compliment.) In the course of our several hour conversation; he said he saw good qualities in me, etc. About the only thing he did not approve of was how short my hair was. (His hangs down over his shoulders.) They both said that they wished I could come up with them to Walla Walla that evening yet, and spend some time getting to know them. Unfortunately, I had to decline, because of returning to Portland on Friday. I did promise to try to make it up to Walla Walla while I am still in the NW. He said he was opening himself up (in us parting ways) to the possibility of my walking away and not wanting any more to do with him. I assured him there was no such thought in my mind. I DO want to get better acquainted. It seems that we have a good, unique relationship started. I personally think there has been the beginning of some real healing begun as a result of all this.

Our conversation sort of tosses away some of the remaining shards of the "father wound" things I had. I had believed my dad did not want me. This was entirely not true. The results of Viet Nam, Agent Orange, the unpopularity of the war, anger issues in general, all contributed. He had cut himself off from hope of seeing me again; cut off any emotions in that regard. I know both of us had to process quite a bit before we were really ready to meet. Whether or not we were entirely ready; it was time. In the providence of God, we met.

He pointed out the bridge he camped out under (just up Emigrant from CSD) when negotiations were in motion to put me up for foster care. An under the bridge living Viet Nam vet /hippie. That is what he was, and in a small way, what he still is.

(At about 4 pm; as it was getting windy, we went over to Big John's Pizza for a bite and what turned out to be over an hour of talk. The extended Bliss family was planning to be there for a Birthday party later on. It was a good place to hang out.)

At Big John's our conversation just got better. My dad and his present wife are admitted "wrecks" saved by the grace of God. She goes to a Foursquare Church. My dad goes once in a while. "Gets his God stuff at the AA" and seems to thrive on telling those around him what God has done in his life. He says he cannot believe, in retrospect, how rotten a life he lived, etc. He says he eventually learned "God wins in the end." I take it for granted that they are Christians…God is leading them in the way to Himself. Christ is doing a good work in them, perhaps despite appearances.

My dad did say, it was quite amazing that we were both sitting across the table from each other, SOBER, and not "needing" to "go get a joint" to cope. As he admitted, there could have been the potential of that happening.

We talked and got acquainted and generally way too much good things happened to be able to record here. A lot of it will come to mind as life goes on. I suppose it will sink in, the huge boatload of GOOD that God allowed me to take in this week.

Chapter 26

So....what happened after all of that?
I am sure you might have begun to see a pattern.
Just what do you mean?
Something good appears to happen or comes to the point of being ready to happen and...
And what?
The "good thing" happened, yes...
So what is with the hesitation?
It was accompanied and followed by enough confusing events that sometimes I wonder if the good ever really happened.
Just how can you dare to say that?
Because nothing really went the way that I expected or... or wanted.
So?
The ironic thing is that I am not even sure I knew what I wanted.
Did you ever find out what you wanted?
Um....
Did you ever find what you wanted?
Gradually, I think.
I suppose I overstayed my welcome out in Oregon.

One morning I got a phone call from Tim Weaver, asking if I would consider coming back and going along on their annual PR trip.

I told him I would think about it.

We hung up.

The next couple of months were a roller coaster that at one point had me contemplating suicide.

I admit that I made a number of "wrong turns".

I probably never should have left Arcola and taken the trip out to Oregon for a "visit" that eventually lasted several months.

I probably shouldn't have done a number of things that I did over that time.

In fact, there are only two good results of the time I spent out there.

I met my real dad.

I was able to be with my adoptive family over the time my adoptive dad passed away.

There is a saying I heard once, that fits right here "good and bad run on parallel tracks, and they both seem to arrive at about the same time."

During the first part of January, mom was gone for a couple of weeks to attend one of her grandchildren's wedding.

I suppose you could say I was alone too long in the house.

I also got blindsided by a string of accusations that were flung at me from someone in the family. Some of them were true…a number of them seemed to be charges that were believed to be so true that my side (if I dared to claim to have a side) were not considered. Or even given a chance to be spoken.

So I listened to the litany of things I had done wrong, and since there was no room or reason to defend myself, I didn't.

I was somewhat ordered to "repent"…show some facial emotion…something to indicate to him that what he had lined me up with was soaking in.

We stood on the porch…him almost furiously trying to get some fitting response out of me…and me getting more and more of a sensation akin to being huddled in a corner waiting for blow to rain upon blow.

There was absolutely no way I could bring myself to allow the tears to come…that were brimming just below the surface.

I felt like I had been shoved past the tipping point.

In the confusion and anger and shame of the moment, I felt powerless to make any "right" decisions.

I went inside after he left and literally snapped.

Whether I cried or not at that point really is beside the point. I threw a huge tantrum. I cursed myself to the devil's hell.

In that moment, I felt like absolute crap…garbage…beyond worthless.

I began thinking seriously about ropes and beams in the shed out back.

Why NOT end it all?

It is actually not really amazing that I did not follow through with these thoughts. The main reasons that kept me from it were what would people think, and it wouldn't do you any good anyway…you know where you would end up, and you don't want to go there.

What is amazing is that a week or two after this, Tim called again.

When we got off the phone, I began to make plans to go back to Fresh Start. For their PR trip to the South that February.

Wisely or unwisely, I said yes.

I was to be gone until the tenth of April.

Three years later...
No words come...
I would love being delightful
And churn out another poem
But no words come.
I would love to ask the reason
For the blossoms
Strewn across dad's
Freshly covered grave
By a random gust of wind
On that clear and yet cold day...
But no words come.
I would love to analyze the ache
That comes, dad, with your memory,
And what was really going on
Inside your mind I would like to ask and see...
But no words come.
So the silent gust of wind
That blew the blossoms from the tree
Perhaps conveys a message
I will one day begin to see...
Tho no words come.

I do not know what to say about the week or so surrounding dad B's death.

Am I supposed to say that I sensed as soon as I got back to Oregon that no one really wanted me back around there?

Probably not.

Am I supposed to say that I felt total freedom to go up to his bed side?

Maybe...unless truth is valued.

I felt no freedom or welcome to go to his bed side.

A number of my siblings were gathered in the room. We, or rather, they, began singing and going up to his bedside for what was probably last goodbyes.

Several of my siblings motioned or nudged me up to the bed side.

I would not. That is the official version, probably. But I am not telling the official version. I could not. It was as if an invisible hand was holding me back. Or a huge thumb was pinning me into position on the floor where I sat with my legs crossed.

Maybe it was just me. Maybe my mind was playing tricks with me. There might be a slight chance that it was for real. I am talking about the look that eventually crossed his face when our eyes finally met.

I eventually made my way to the foot of the bed.

And our eyes met.

The look that I have been told I imagined on his face made my heart sink.

I had seen that look many times growing up.

It was a look of disapproval.

This, real or imagined, plunged me even further into a sort of withdrawing from the others.

I also made the mistake of relating what I saw, or thought I saw, to mom. I know, it was the worst possible thing and at the worst possible time.

I made a lot of other mistakes that week as well. Such as clamming up when my sister in law and I were on the way to the nursing home the following morning. She wanted me to "process" by talking about dad and things. There was absolutely no way I could start talking without coming totally unglued...which, I knew was absolutely not permitted.

At least that is what all of my experience in the family up to that point had told me.

It did not take very long to get rebuked for loading mom up with the outrageous lies I was telling about what I claimed to see on dad's face.

I was also roundly rebuked by one of my older brothers for not showing more emotion.

I went into my room and wept for about forty-five minutes. Which he never found out about, and as far as I was concerned, he had no business ever finding out about.

I am not sure if I had ever felt so alone...misunderstood...hated....in my life, as I did at that point.

I am not going to go into a lot more details, except to say that I was commanded to be strong for mom and the rest of the family's sake. And, since I knew all about putting on appearances, and how you are supposed to appear when you are being that sort of "strong"...I managed.

The only tears I shed in public were at dad's grave side, during the committal prayer. The only reason I allowed the few tears was the hope that my tinted lenses on my glasses would hide the fact that I was crying.

I had a severe migraine headache the day of the funeral. I eventually was able to get some pain reliever and got through the day.

We were almost ready to leave the cemetery, when a gust of wind blew some blossoms off a tree close to the freshly covered grave.

Chapter 27

About a year after I left Fresh Start at the termination of my first term, I was back. Probably not fit to be there, certainly not fit to be a counsellor, and barely, it would turn out, fit to be a shop assistant.

For a while life was somewhat comfortable at Fresh Start. At least on the surface. I was a shop assistant the second time around. This was mostly by mutual agreement...I could see no way I would be able to pretend to be a counsellor again. Especially not after the harrowing year I had gone through between my terms there.

The ones in charge at Fresh Start apparently agreed. I somewhat secretly went back to Fresh Start more for my own good than for any benefit I would have been able to bring to the Fresh Start program.

So...although maybe it was a well intentioned mistake all around, I wound up back at Fresh Start. I managed to avoid some turbulent events that were rocking the system. At least for a while.

Before getting totally engulfed in Fresh Start again, I was allowed to go to SMBI for a six week term. In a way it was almost a waste of my time. I came back to Fresh Start and was promptly flung into conflict upon conflict and very nearly impassable tests were forced upon me.

There are a thousand "I should haves try to condemn me as I write this. Any evidence of spiritual growth in my life seemed to be ignored, snuffed out or discounted.

There were a couple times at SMBI during that one term that I was convinced that I felt the presence of the Spirit of God moving on me and showing His love to me.

Once I got back to Fresh Start, I got almost no encouragement to continue my growth in grace.

I was confronted by what I was certain were false accusations. It seemed every intention of my heart being called into question. It eventually became clear that either I had made a huge mistake coming back to Fresh Start...or that it was simply time for me to leave.

Possibly, both.

I gradually realized that I could no longer uphold as true a number of "key" Mennonite beliefs. At the same time, hints were being thrown my way that I should begin thinking about getting back into a counselor role at Fresh Start. "With your experiences and what you know and your insights into life, you should let us groom you to be a Fresh Start counselor."

I was being compelled to draw some "different" conclusions regarding the "mode" of baptism. I began realize that when I was baptized into the Mennonite Church, I was not born again. One of my mentors tried to convince me that I was, and that my doubts were evidence of listening to lies. But in my spirit, the logic trail was simple and direct. I wasn't born again when I was "baptized" with a handful of water at age 19. I allowed my love of words and meanings to propel me into studying what baptize actually means. And the definitions I encountered sealed the question for me. I had definitely not been submerged, engulfed, or overwhelmed in water. Whatever I had submitted to was not a baptism.

I knew that requesting rebaptism by pouring was not an option. The Mennonite church I was a member of at Fresh Start would probably not even consider immersing me. So I did not even bother to ask.

I promised God, if you lead me to some people who would immerse me, I would do it.

Eventually I was forced to make the almost impossible choice. There were some things being emphasized that amounted to glorified self effort. There was very little about being born again or being in the Kingdom of God or any evidence of being endowed with the Spirit of God. There was a lot of emphasis on accountability to the point of relying on an "accountability person" and almost no indication of belief in the Spirit of God.

There was also the tendency to require someone in authority to be elevated to an almost God status. It was demanded that those "under authority" confess their sins and short comings to those who were "in authority" over them. With the added assumption that for the authority figure to confess in any way to those "under" him would equal destroying his "authority". Authority figures "confessing to each other" is apparently okay. But they must never confess to their inferiors the way their inferiors confess to them.

The day they did that, it was declared, was the day their authority disappeared.

I could not pretend to believe that was true.

There were several meetings in which some of these issues were discussed. In the course of events I was no longer able to "hide out in shop". I was driven to a point of having to speak my mind. And it cost me. A lot.

One morning during a staff meeting, I blurted out that I was having a hard time reconciling lording it over the men in the program with what the Bible says about the example of Jesus as described in Philippians 2. I could not see how I could command the men in the program to follow the example of Jesus in humbling Himself while we as "authorities" were refusing to do it ourselves.

I was shocked by the almost livid reaction those several sentences aroused. "Are you trying to destroy the Fresh Start authority structure?" my mentor asked.

I could not understand the totally stone faced anger in the eyes and faces of the men around the table.

"I've just been reading in the Word and just struggle to see how lording it over men we are not doing very well in relating to is following the example of Christ. If that is destroying the FS authority structure, then I guess so be it."

That morning all the men, staff, and those in the program, had a meeting to try to work through some issues that the men had with the staff. The results over the next several days was disastrous.

That weekend, I agonized over my options.

Monday morning, with a great deal of fear and trembling I went to the front office where the assistant administrator was working. We had a few words. I informed him that I was not at all at peace with how the latest meeting (which included the staff and resident men) had been conducted.

I served him my six month notice.

Meanwhile, my childhood favorite preacher passed away out in Oregon. A friend of mine, who wanted to see the West, went on a flying trip out to Oregon with me.

That was a full week. A funeral. An evening and most of the day at the coast. A run up to Walla Walla, Washington to look up my dad and step mom. On the way up to Walla Walla, we spur of the moment stopped in Pendleton and I dropped in on my Aunt Kathy "for about five minutes" which stretched into forty-five or more. We spent the night and the next morning in Walla Walla and I got to know my dad a little bit more.

We made our way back to Estacada and the next morning flew back to Indianapolis.

Sometime during the first part of May, my sister Sonya passed away.

By Memorial Day, things had come to such a head that there was yet another meeting.

In response to a question, I said "it seems we have accountabilitied the Holy Spirit out of the Fresh Start program."

There was no reason to pretend we were on the same page. I was offered, and accepted, to resign and leave the next day.

Memorial Day there was a softball game and carry in at the church.

By Tuesday evening I had my stuff packed and loaded up and my friend from Illinois was nice enough to come over to Daviess County and bring me back to Arcola.

And, so, my years at Fresh Start came to an end.

Chapter 28

For a number of months I did not attend church anywhere. I felt my self more or less led into a wilderness. Part of that wilderness included having it out with only God and myself.

I am not sure if I would recommend doing this to just anyone. However, it may be healthy once in a while to get away from systems and religion and all that is involved in church and find out where your own feet stand.

After the experiences of the previous year or so, I needed to do just that. So I sort of allowed myself to drop off the map for almost a whole summer.

Around August, I "came back around" and told a friend of mine (neither of us were attending any where at the time) "I don't know about you, but I need to fellowship with somebody...somewhere."

I knew of some ex Amish families who were meeting as a small group up the road from where I lived. One weekend, almost spur of the moment, I decided to "break my church fast" and meet with these folks who met in the basement of one of their houses.

By the time the service was over, I knew I had found the group God wanted me to fellowship with.

Several months later, someone mentioned that "a couple of the girls in our group are going to get baptized in a couple of weeks."

My heart skipped a beat.
I asked if I would be able to be baptized also.
So it was arranged.

In the meantime, a number of emails passed between me and the ministry at Fresh Start. I informed them that I considered myself no longer part of the Mennonite system. Eventually they did due process and I received a letter informing me that my membership was revoked.

After I received the letter, which was the equivalent of a church letter and included some words about what kind of a person I was, I first printed it out. I was not really sure what I should do with it. Should I archive it?

I decided to take a cue from what the men in the Fresh Start Program did when they shared their life story.

I burned the letter. And felt an immense weight drop from my spirit.

I had come to Arcola in what must have looked like insane obedience.

I had obeyed the illogical looking nudge to get immersed. And I knew it meant severing some more Mennonite ties.

Meanwhile, I had been doing some serious study on the baptism of the Holy Spirit. And I was plodding through some intense personal issues of my own.

I would read and then try to pray. Sometimes I would be able to pray through and get a sense of release in some areas. But I seemed to be blocked. I knew what I wanted. I had longed for it desperately...but it seemed just out of reach. It was almost as if someone was trying to keep me from receiving the next thing God had for me.

It would take the arrival of a frankly unpopular preacher who would come with a foundation shaking series of meetings at a nearby Mennonite church.

The week of Good Friday saw a number of tornado watches come through the area. There was also a spiritual earthquake, and it came in the form of a preacher named Wayne.

He preached night after night from the altar at the foot of the pulpit. Because God told him to, in order to break down any spiritual resistance that had built up as a result of years of preaching the wisdom of man and tradition that denied the power of God.

One night there was a tornado warning.

Several nights people in the audience were healed of various illnesses.

Then came Good Friday.

It was a gloomy, cloudy morning, even for the area. By eleven o'clock in the morning it still looked like early morning...or twilight.

When I awoke that morning I was in such physical pain that I could barely get out of bed. I have frequently had severe migraine headaches, and I think that is what it was.

I finally was able to get up and after a while we went to the laundromat to do laundry...bachelor style.

Meanwhile, my head...every part of my body, actually... was throbbing. I felt light headed and it was all I could do to stand upright. Let alone have a conversation with anyone. The slightest noise was enough to almost drive me out of my mind.

We went across town to get a bite to eat, and I managed to keep down some food.

That afternoon, there was going to be a meeting for anyone who was interested to join in a time of sharing, fellowship, or whatever would occur.

My friend decided to go. I was riding on the strength of pain relievers at that point and decided to stay at the house and try to regain my strength so as to be able to go to the evening service.

Since I was not there, I am not going to try to say what all happened in that meeting. I will say, the Holy Spirit powerfully showed up.

Meanwhile, approximately three in the afternoon, I started to feel well enough to get up and get a shower and slowly get ready to go to the meeting.

The thought crossed my mind. What if something happens over at the church this afternoon and you aren't there to see it? Will you be able to believe it is from Me, and will you be able to accept that it happened without you being there?

I knew it was God asking those questions.

The words of Jesus flashed into my mind. Blessed is he who did not see, and yet believed.

"Yes, Father," I said, somewhat mystified.

At about six I got a text from my friend "The Holy Spirit visited us."

I was totally unprepared for what I saw that evening in the meeting. I could barely comprehend the change that had come over my friend. There was every evidence that it was real... and I was honestly afraid of what I saw.

The service eventually came to a close. We all went home.

My friend and I sat in the car, he was talking full speed ahead about what had happened that afternoon and what was happening in him even then.

When there was a pause in what he was saying, I turned to him and said, "Do you have any idea how long I have waited to see something like this?"

"No," he said, "I probably don't. You have probably waited and wanted it longer than most of the rest of us."

After a while we got out of the car and went into the house. My friend began doing what he called "spiritual house cleaning."

I went into my room in sort of a daze. To be honest, I was jealous, just a little bit. I knew I had told God I was fine with not being on hand when the others had received the visitation of the Spirit. But I wanted it in the worst way.

With a pounding heart I went over to the living room where my friend was sitting.

"Okay, I'm ready."

Before long I was face down on the floor. At first the words would not come. Then I began praying and repenting and confessing attitudes and sins of the spirit that I did not even know were there. That night their presence and power loomed large.

After several agonizing moments, I was able to utter the words, "God, I forgive you for all the crap that I have blamed you for causing in my life." This opened the gates of my spirit and I began to pray and forgive yet again...a long string of people.

As the Spirit brought names and faces to mind, I said, "yes, I forgive them....and them...and them..."

I prayed in this manner, going extremely deep into a lot of painful areas.

Until we hit a road block.

The scene at my adoptive dad's bed side came into my mind, unbidden. (I was crying uncontrollably by this time.) Still face down, on the floor, I envisioned myself at the Father's feet. "God, did I make all that stuff up....about dad?!" I was sobbing uncontrollably and pounding the floor with my fists as I asked this. "If I made it up...load me up with condemnation... or something. I need to know."

Somewhere along the line I asked...begged...demanded, the Spirit. I was more desperate than I had ever remembered being in my life.

I lay on my face for several minutes. Waiting for what would come.

The only way I know to describe it as, is a sad peace came over me. I sensed the Father telling me, "We both know you didn't make it up. All the things you have remembered...they have been true." He had one other word for me. "But I was there, all the time, even when you didn't know it."

About this time, I began feeling what I can only describe as a hot tingling sensation starting in my hands and gradually going all through me.

"God, I don't know if this is the baptism of the Holy Spirit or not, whatever this is that is coming on me. But if it is, give it to me and I will accept it."

I felt myself immediately engulfed in the power of the Spirit and love of God.

I felt my mouth begin moving and making words that I did not understand. It began as a bit of a dribble. But then suddenly...

I knew I had received the sign gift of tongues. My friend said later that I appeared to him to be in a sort of trance, although I was totally aware of what was going on around me. According to my friend, I kept on speaking, or praying, in tongues for over an hour.

At one point, my friend said, "God, you are giving him a language to speak to You directly from his spirit. And I will not speak against it."

When I heard him say that, what was going on "clicked" inside my mind. Even so, I found myself wondering if I was making this all up.

I attempted to form English words. But it was as if the Father said, "Nope, you aren't going to talk English until I let you."

The conversation in tongues, with God, lasted apparently over an hour. I am sure my spirit and the Spirit of God had some dealings about some deep seated things.

At one point, all at once, I began laughing...as if my spirit had attained a measure of release and freedom.

I finally got up off the floor and went to my room, my mouth still bypassing my natural understanding and conversing with God in tongues.

I looked over at my friend and motioned that I would talk like normal if I could, but I couldn't.

Finally, (it was around two in the morning by this time) it began to subside.

I was "given" the English language back, again.

The first English words out of my mouth were a long string of thank you's.

Several evenings later, it occurred to me that I HAD been given an actual prayer language. I could use it to talk to the Father, direct.

So I wrote the following praise poem:

Father of my Lord Jesus Christ,
Thank you for this
Incredible,
Supernatural,
Unexplainable
Gift of your Spirit.
You have given me a "language"
To speak directly to you
In the Spirit.

You have given...
And promised...
The ability to interpret
What you have given me to say
In the Spirit as well.
Thanks, and glory be to you
For this stunning,
Incredible,
Gift of grace.
Do not
Question it
Look back
Doubt it
Walk in what God has given you by His Spirit.

Chapter 29

God sometimes lets His children get into situations where they look and feel perfectly stupid.

Or at least it sometimes feels like it. Maybe it is just our own human folly allowed to manifest itself so it can be exposed as the hindrance and subtle enemy of our walk with God. And maybe, even if we are walking in the Light and living in the Spirit, there is more and more pride and humanity and self will that has to be exposed and dealt with.

So we are allowed to walk into some devastating valleys, that are absolutely confusing, and that kills and shakes everything but that part of us that is desperately longing for God. And sometimes we get to the point of wondering if any of that stuff...that seemed so real...so close to God...so perfect and close to heaven...was actually true. Life goes on and a day comes that we wonder if it really happened.

I do not know why such devastating doubt often follows such moments and days of certainty...unless it to see if we are trusting in the experience with God or the God who gave the experience. Perhaps it is so we actually see more of ourselves.

I may not know why, but I do know it happens. And it can be devastating when it does. Devastating in a bad way, and at the same time, devastating in a good way, that is not visible until afterward. Devastating to the pride...to the wild desire to look right and be right and (finally, after searching for it) actually feel right.

> *I've read about you...*
> *heard about you*
> *Seen all the data*
> *That has been compiled*
> *And have made up my mind*
> *In a thousand ways...*
> *That I know everything*
> *There is to know about you...*
> *I knew too much*
> *To be fooled*
> *by an appearance*
> *of the real YOU...*
> *Then suddenly*
> *YOU stood there*
> *In the door...*
> *The data and the*
> *Knowledge*
> *I had compiled*
> *Semed like a child's fancy*
> *And a shadow...*
> *Nothing more...*
> *'Cause the real*
> *YOU was standing*
> *In the door...*

There is a guy I met via Facebook whose name is Harvey. I had heard of him...a little, anyway. I knew he was a writer, but besides that, I knew almost nothing about him.

One morning I woke up depressed.

For no real reason I turned on my computer, got on line and got on Facebook.

I was aimlessly...almost mindlessly...browsing.

On a fb friend's status, I saw "Harvey Yoder likes this".

I thought..."Not THE Harvey, surely? The one who wrote all these books..."

As stupid as it seemed to me, I messaged this guy...

You don't know me that I know of, but I have heard a lot about you and I think I have read a number of your books. I am a sort of amateur writer. I am in the middle of a life story project that may interest you.

To my shock he messaged me back, almost immediately.

Cool. Where do you live? Wanna be friends?

This was totally not what I expected.

Um, sure...if he wanted to.

We started chatting, and slowly he drew out of me some of the story of the past couple of months.

I do not trust anyone very easily...but he seemed real enough...and safe enough...and, well, just drew it right out of me...gradually.

Suddenly, the almost unbelievable happened.

I was getting prophesied over...I watched in stunned silence as words...paragraphs...filled the chat box. Words that are too sacred and too personal and too many to put here.

"...You have been questioning about something in your life and not knowing what to do about it, but God is tell you it is OK, He knows about it and you can safely let Him take care of it....You have wanted to know how to "overcome" and have tried, but the Lord tells you to stop all the trying. He will do in your heart what He alone can do. Do not fret, but let Him love on you and as you look into His eyes of love and know you are

perfectly understood and loved, your heart will continue to be filled with praise and awe for Him."

It was all I could do to allow myself to read those words... let alone know what to do with them. I could almost not grasp that God would tell anyone...and someone who I did not even know, for that matter...to tell me things like that...things that I desperately needed and wanted to hear...and almost believed that I would never hear.

Why...why...why would God say this to...me?

"...Satan had thought he had you all bound up and tied in knots and you wondered if you could face life and suddenly you are finding out that Jesus really has made you and created you just the way He wanted to and He is proud to call you Son. You no longer need to bow in shame, but you will lift your face towards heaven and walk boldly and with confidence. People who have despised you will stand back in wonder and see the change and instead of pointing fingers, your life will point them to Jesus..."

I was...dumbfounded. I had never...ever...dreamed anyone would say anything like this to me.

Then I saw these words appear in the chat box: *"Joshua, get up and raise your hands towards heaven and shout, I am a Friend of God! I am made in His image and I rejoice in who I am! I am a friend of God! I refuse to let shame and lies drag me down."*

I could not do any of that. Perhaps I was too emotionally locked down. I wanted to believe it...but it seemed beyond... reality, really. At least the reality that I could see.

God wanted me to "safely trust Him to take care of it...?" really? I was "perfectly understood?" Really? No one anywhere close to me came close to even trying to understand me, let alone actually claiming to.

I was barely able to believe that "God was proud of me and called me son". It was almost all I could do to whisper...almost above my breath, "I am a friend of God."

None of it felt real...I could not understand how any of it could be real...especially since my spirit...or was it my soul... maybe it was and maybe it wasn't...felt...numb.

Numb as in, numbed by fear.

At the time I was surrounded by people who were obsessed with "doing it right"...having to make sure everything was "just right" before anything could be entered into. You were allowed to share in the meeting if you qualified...which means it was totally obvious to the leaders that you were living in as much of the Spirit as they allowed for, denounced the "religiousness" of those around us, bemoaned the fact that "we" were persecuted and were the only ones that were even close to being the Kingdom.

There is very little about me that fits in with "doing it right". I showed entirely too much "flesh" and not enough "fruit of the Spirit" to convince the leaders that I was ever even born again, much less had a real "baptism in the Spirit". This was because they were not on hand to witness it, and therefore they were not able to control the experience or the manifestations, or the outcome.

They also emphasized "loud voiced denouncing of the sins of the too religious" and other perceived aspects of the "prophetic gift" that I refused to act as if I have. So I was suspect in the eyes of these who proclaimed that my failure to "proclaim and defame" was an indication that I was refusing to walk into my "prophetic gift."

I also really had no desire to control or grasp leadership over anyone. And further more, I refused to accept the idea that prevailed in the group that "we are the only ones."

All of this was in the background of meeting Harvey via Facebook.

I mentioned that I was planning to attend a weekend conference in PA, and after some thought, Harvey said he and his wife might go to that conference as well.

I had been more or less jobless since leaving Fresh Start. I had picked up a part time job at a cabinet shop, sanding drawer parts and some assembly. But the work was getting slow, and my friend, who I had been rooming with also had his hours cut back by a lot.

So I began the almost hopeless...nearly fruitless task of filling out applications and making phone calls and...waiting.

One day, someone suggested that I try to get a job at CHI, the garage door factory just outside of Arthur. There didn't seem to be any other options, and I had no idea how any of this would work out, so I went online and filled out an application with Select Remedy, who hired temporary workers on behalf of CHI.

To my amazement, I got a phone call asking for an appointment for an interview.

A day or two later I went down to CHI, had the interview, and in spite of Craig's almost negative...and what turned out to be accurate...assessment that I looked too timid for what an assembly line job required, they decided to give me a chance.

I was supposed to start July 25.

But before that, there was a quick trip to Pennsylvania with some friends to attend a weekend conference. I was more or less "on the defensive" and had all my guards up when we went to the conference in PA.

On one side, the trip was almost a waste of time. The new job I was supposed to be starting Monday was fearfully seared in my mind. I more or less got nothing out of it.

Except that Harvey and his wife showed up at the meeting and we met, very briefly. At the time it did not make any sense why I was there, or why they were there. Except that for reasons that only God knew we were supposed to meet each other.

So the long hours on the road and the conference that leaned more toward teaching than anything else was not quite totally lost time.

I was supposed to begin work the next day, Monday. When we got back, I stayed the night at a friend's place, because the CHI van was going to come by around six in the morning.

We got back to the house at about 2 in the morning. So I had about three hours at the most to sleep.

Strong coffee and a couple of Monster kept me going most of that day.

The first week or so I was kept busy trying to keep up in the hardware department, counting out hinges to put into boxes to be shipped with each garage doors.

I sweated, and struggled, and swore under my breath and tried desperately to keep up, and remember almost a thousand and one things.

It did not go terrible, although I could have said it did. I instinctively sensed that in spite of my best efforts I was holding up the line.

So I would go home, mentally and physically exhausted.

The first day of the third week I was there I was sent over to the Springs department. The work was quite a bit more varied, and a lot harder, but for the most part I enjoyed it. And I hoped that maybe this would last longer than "just" a couple of weeks or a month or something.

We even looked for an apartment in town. Mysteriously, there seemed to be nothing available. So it was decided that I would rent a room from Paul in his basement until I could find an apartment or until something came up.

As it happened, I worked at CHI just under a month. I am not sure if I actually got warning signs that I was soon going to be let go. There was a week or so that they had unusually short days, and that might have had a bit to do with being let go.

I was mostly convinced it had something, a lot, maybe, with not really being fast enough, or strong enough, or something enough.

One afternoon, as we were cleaning up close to quitting time, the boss of the factory called me over and in the nicest, "Amishest" way possible said, "I am sorry, it is not going to work out. We are going to have to let you go."

I managed to stammer a "Um, thank you for the opportunity." And walked away...fired.

I tried hard not to be angry, but I did not succeed very well in the attempt. In fact, I proved to at least one person that I was not very spiritually mature...and gave him every cause to question if I was ever, or for real even born again.

I felt betrayed. I had put my trust in God...and had followed the advice of others that led to getting this job. And just about the time it seemed that I had God's blessing on it...it fell apart.

I wasn't supposed to feel betrayed by God if I was totally committed and believed in my heart that God was good and looking out for my good. I felt betrayed. I wasn't supposed to doubt or question what God was doing. I doubted and questioned. I wasn't supposed to "show flesh" and show anger, frustration, bitterness, doubt. I was angry...I was frustrated...I fought bitterness and swam in doubt.

I wanted desperately to be able to throw all of out...and yet I didn't. I was torn between belief and doubt in ways I had never been before this. I could not leave...although I wanted to...kind of. I wanted to believe...but it...hurt too much to. It also hurt too much not to.

In the middle of all of this I was given (if that is the right word) a prophetic poem.

I was sprawled out on my bed...thinking and not wanting to think...a very dangerous and possibly explosive state of mind to be in. A fertile seed bed for...anything.

I stared at the paper.

"Afraid." I wrote.

Afraid....
Afraid to love...
Afraid of grace.

Gulp. I hated where this seemed to be going.

In a matter of minutes I had scrawled the rest of the lines:

Afraid to see whats on His face.
Afraid that I'll be sent away...
Afraid to hope He'll bid me stay.
Afraid to fling myself on grace...
Or to believe there is a place
Within His heart for such as I.
Afraid He'll scold me if I cry.
The door is shut...
Dark is the room...
Face to the wall
Heart full of gloom...
There almost is no hope in sight...

There are no brilliant words or light.
There is nothing...
Just a quiet sense...
I don't want him here...
But I feel his presence.
Tho my splintered heart
Screams Why don't you leave?
He stays with a grace
I almost cannot believe.
My spirit screams
I hate you, God!
I sense an understanding nod
As if He knows
I am in too much pain...
He leaves with a promise
To come back again.
My spirit soars
But my will is weak...
I sense Him say to my heart:
Lay back and be still
Don't even try to speak...
Don't even try to understand...
Or comprehend My will.
This is all you need to know:
You are my Child still.

I stared at what I had just written. I almost could not believe I wrote it. In all honesty, I did not feel like I even believed it. I felt like a hypocrite...except that something undefinable inside of me wildly wanted it to be true.

But was it?

Was any of it true?

Had any of this "stuff" I thought was real...really happened?

Was I really...born again? Was getting immersed really the right decision that it seemed to be at the time?

Was...it even real? Had I made it all up? Was I trying to make it up, even now?

Had I really been baptized in the Spirit?

It is astounding how many questions pounded my heart and spirit in the following couple weeks.

In the middle of all this, on top of losing my job at CHI, the job I had at the cabinet shop threatened to go from part time to almost nothing.

You are supposed to trust God without question, right? Especially if you are supposed to be "filled with the Spirit" and think you are walking in the Spirit, right? There is no room for doubts or second guesses of any kind...right?

Well...I questioned, and doubted, and second guessed a lot...even in the middle of trying to live a life that was "filled with the Spirit" and claiming to be walking in the Spirit.

Meanwhile, I got an email from an unexpected place. It was unexpected because I had contacted them about a year or so before this and had told them to keep me in mind if they needed any one on their writing/editing team. It was a publishing house in TN called Lighthouse Publishing that publishes a periodic magazine by and for prison inmates.

I had just been informed that there would not be much more work in the weeks ahead.

I was sitting in the garage, a combination of moping and trying to collect my thoughts. What in the world am I going to do? No job...no real reason to be anywhere close to thinking about hanging around here in Arcola. No real signal that I am supposed to leave, either. God, WHAT am I supposed to do?

I could not believe the next random thought that came to mind. Check your email. NOW.

Shrug. Why not? I could think of better ideas...and there were stupider ideas.

So I checked my email.

And could not believe my eyes.

"Are you still interested in working with Lighthouse?"

Um, Yeah...Of course I was.

I shot back an email, telling them that I was...very interested.

"We do have one question. Would you be donating your time, or would you like a small wage?"

God, what am I supposed to say?

Did I almost sense a divine...smirk? "Say whatever you want to say."

Gulp. Really? Ok.

I replied that I would appreciate a small wage.

"How would ten dollars an hour sound?"

I was...astounded. It was not going to be full time, and it would be somewhat sporadic...but at least I would be able to survive.

And it would be getting paid for something that I actually enjoyed and was even able to do...a lot better than some other things I had tried.

And I could do it where ever I could set up a laptop and have access to internet.

So, all of a sudden I was almost unbelievingly ecstatic.

I was actually able to do something I knew a little bit about...and enjoyed...and get paid a little for doing it? Wow. It was hard to believe, but it was true.

Meanwhile, there was a road trip to a little place in Pennsylvania for a little thing called The Gathering.

My friend and I both agreed that we should go...but we were not really agreed on whether to drive or fly.

One evening, as we were both in our rooms, doing our things, he blurted out: "I have been thinking and looking for airline tickets. I think we should fly out to PA."

Just as quickly, I blurted, "I don't think we are supposed to fly."

Um...ok. He assumed that I was afraid to fly, which was not entirely true. But I did not bother trying to press the issue that he was wrong or why he was wrong or why I got this sense that we were simply not supposed to fly.

I did not know why we weren't supposed to...I just sensed that we weren't.

Meanwhile, I had friended someone on facebook who I had known when we were both kids in Oregon.

We spent a lot of time on fb chat...trying to figure each other out...seeing if it was possible to come close to trusting each other...clawing at each other as it were and fighting our way to at least a semblance of mutual respect.

It happened that the weekend we were going out to PA, this person was heading out to Illinois.

We half chatted, half joked about maybe getting our paths to cross in some way...in Ohio, or somewhere in Pa. This person lived in PA, and as things occurred, our paths crossed in a little town of Washington, PA.

In the course of texting back and forth on the road, we figured out where we were in relation to each other and met at a McDonalds and talked for a few brief minutes.

We soon were on our way to the Gathering again. I blurted "...I think I just found out why we were not supposed to fly."

My friend, who was driving...and becoming less and less sure that he was even supposed to be heading to the Gathering to begin with, said, "Why? What do you mean? I still think it would have been a better idea to fly."

"That 'chance meeting' back there, was one of the reasons." I said.

"Um....Oka......y."

There might be no good way to describe that weekend, which proved to be way too short.

I will attempt to describe it by quoting something I wrote soon after we got back to Illinois.

An incredible worship team from the Church in Baltimore
(You guys ARE amazing!)
And powerful words from Penn...
(If you are reading this, Penn, I love your accent)
Twenty four hours in the presence of God
...adoring...
worshipping...
...dancing before Him...
...feeling His love for maybe the first time
Arms outstretched...
...hands raised to heaven...
I kind of feel like a tree...finally coming to life.
Suddenly four guys are around me
Praying...prophesying into my life...
"Let it out...release it...release it"
Suddenly realizing that you were praying so in the Spirit that you did not even realize when they left...
And actually feeling His presence.
Not just knowing He is here.
Not just imagining yourself in his arms...
HIM ACTUALLY BEING THERE...and you can feel it.
If this is worship...I could never get tired of it.
My spirit is finally home.

It is almost unbelievable to hear someone say he is inspired to worship...by me
Lots of things that seem impossible are true.
Receive the honor that people give you. Then when you are alone with God, give it to Him.
being spoken over and having the word confirmed three different ways
by different people saying variations of the same things...
AND KNOWING IT WAS TRUE IS FROM GOD AND FOR YOU.
Because they know nothing about you...where you are from, where you have been or what the desires of your heart are...
And it hit home, directly.
Painfully (it hurts to hear some of the longings and visions of your heart called out and validated)
Beautifully (Maybe I am finally seeing what everyone has seen for a long time)
Incredibly (except...it happened. what I had longed for... forever...finally got a taste...ah, what a taste!)
Openly (there is no way to hide or go back to what was... not now)
Thank you Abba for a prayer language and the liberty to use it!
...feeling selfish for doing a whole lot of receiving and yet being told that is all you are supposed to do
...receive. Receive. RECEIVE.
Ok. I receive it.
Does it really show on my face????
Awesome fellowship over meals...
And more fellowship over snacks...
...six inches of snow...
flickering lights...

"does that make sense?" "you spoke way more than you know" moments

...worship and dancing before God
I can't dance
Says who?
I never have
You can start tonight
Dancing before God is a release of joy...and it is also how you receive joy
There is an old man in the back who is out doing all of you younger ones
Ok...thats a dare.
It is awesome to dance
...listening to perfectly awesome God stories
...wondrous deliverances
Yes...Yes...Yes..it is incredible when you can join the most radical Christians you have ever met in praying for release... on behalf of others...in the language of the Spirit...
AND SEE THE VISIBLE RESULTS
And having powerhouse prayer warriors, pray and prophesy over you...confirming beyond what you have heard...
THEN...
THEN...
...a spontaneous communion service
Ok...never mind it was tea and hot dog buns...
we feasted before Christ...no we feasted with Him...no...we were served by Him...
Listened to songs of intimacy with Jesus...
...did I mention I am "wasted"
...and maybe I will learn how to dance...and way, way more...

So we left that Sunday morning and went to Petra. We planned to leave much before we did, but

We finally left around two in the afternoon...and had twelve to fourteen hours of driving ahead of us. On ridiculously little sleep. You could say we were literally riding on the fumes of the Spirit.

We were standing around after church in the auditorium, talking. All of a sudden, my friend blurted out, "I just want to get rid of everything, and...go."

Almost that quick, I said, "Maybe we should go to Harvey's."

Neither of us really say that one coming.

By the time we got back to Illinois it seemed clear that we were supposed to pull up stakes and move. What we would do down in NC, we hardly knew. What God had in mind, we almost had no clue. But it was clear...at least most of the time... that we had been told to move.

The reasons would become apparent...later.

Since there were hours and hours of driving and only the two of us in the car, we talked about a lot of stuff. Our impressions of the Gathering and lots of other things.

As usually happens when guys talk for any length of time, the subject of girls came up. And whether God really called anyone to single-hood, and if God would really give such a thing as male masculinity and in the same breath forbid a guy to fulfill the drives and desires that seemed to go along with this thing...was it a curse or a blessing...called human masculinity.

In the middle of it all my friend suddenly got a "word" for me in relation to a certain girl.

The "word" more or less turned at least ten years of a long conversation with God on this subject on its head. I was hearing that God suddenly decided (or I have always been wrong about what I thought I had heard from Him) to change His mind and that a certain girl was "willing whenever I was ready" to take the plunge to ask her for a deeper relationship.

We were on our way back from a Gathering where I had heard from God...explicitly...and from several different people...and the messages all matched. I had a taste of the real thing. I had even been allowed to express myself in what probably amount to spiritual baby talk...in tongues...for the first time that weekend.

I knew what real felt like, and sounded like, and how it affected me.

What I heard from my friend did not feel, sound like, or affect me like the real thing I had experienced all weekend long. I could not accept it. I fought it, and in the confinement of the car and in the lateness of the hour it felt as if I was fighting God and someone who was convinced he had a word from God...for me.

But...my spirit would not allow me to buy any of it.

My friend continued to "hear from God" on my behalf... things like "she will be willing when you ask her." and such like.

There was one small problem, well maybe two.

I was actually texting the girl he thought God was telling him was "the one" for me. I was more or less trying to be an "older brother" at her request. And we were almost to the point of being able to trust each other on this level.

Then this bombshell changed everything.

I texted the girl something to the effect that I seemed to be hearing from God that she might be the one and that based on that I might be considering pursuing something more than just a casual "brother-sister" type of friendship.

I told her things were such...I seemed to be hearing such huge contradictions...that I had to break off any contact for a while (I set it at a month)..."radio silence" because I had to know what was really going on.

Since this caught us both by total surprise, she was really hesitant to agree. But she saw my point and we agreed to almost no contact.

We finally arrived back in Illinois early Monday morning. And for probably obvious reasons I came down with a cold that was almost flu like and that persisted for almost two weeks.

Meanwhile, we began the crazy business of getting ready to leave the flat lands of Illinois and moving to a small town in the Blue Ridge Mountains of NC called Spruce Pine. And the reason, and in part the "drawing card" was a man I had only met twice before that...and the second time was the weekend of the Gathering.

Around the time of the gathering it was mentioned that I ought to consider going to IHOP in Kansas City for the end of the year One Thing Conference.

So I more or less thought I would somehow get from NC to Kansas City and (again, somehow) figure out what I was supposed to do in KC.

One morning while still in Arcola, I got "a word". It will be told you there what you must do.

I took this to mean that I would be told what to do once I got to Kansas City.

And I figured that since Harvey's were going to Kansas City, it would naturally follow that I could "just" go with them.

But first we had to somehow get to NC...and in a short period of time try to figure out where we were going to live and any occupation or what we were going to do.

The where we were going to live took care of itself...at least temporarily....about a day before we were supposed to move down.

There is a small church called the Bridge Church in Spruce Pine.

Once in NC it became clear that I was not going to be able to go to IHOP. I was more than mildly confused. I replayed the word that I thought had indicated that I was going to go to KC. And slowly, and in spite of my best attempts to convince God and myself otherwise, it began to dawn on me that I would be told in Spruce Pine what I must do.

You will be told there what you must do.

God, you mean, here...in this little...although incredible... town of Spruce Pine?

Sometimes the silence of God is louder and more profound than any ear pleasing, or as the case may have been, ear maddening, answer.

Ok...God...I give up. So I am not supposed to go.

Once that was settled...the next question was...Ok, now what?

Now what turned out to be a lot different from I imagined.

It was a "little side hike" with God that would almost crush me.

The day I thought I was supposed to be in Kansas City at OneThing, I was pounding out nails in a pile of lumber in a huge building called the Colosseum.

And fighting a lifetime of lies.

And inwardly screaming...at God (for leading me wrong)... at myself (for being so stupid)...at...

You were not ready to go to something like OneThing.

Wow.

Suddenly the fight for my life was on.

My mind generated all sort of interpretations for that one. And the Enemy supplied a legion of meanings that seemed to fit into everything life had taught me...or I thought life had taught me.

"You are not good enough."

"You do not deserve it."

"What right did you think you...you...YOU...had to go to something like that?"

"Who did you think you are?"

Literally every lie that has had a voice in my life raised its head that morning.

There was only one thing that kept me from flying all to pieces...a word that I had received in my spirit the day it became clear that I would not be going to Kansas City.

Do not kill desire just because you cannot have what you desire.

What was that supposed to mean?

That morning, in the former music room in the colosseum, pounding nails out of two by fours, it was my only defense against a barrage of lies...vicious lies. And my only protection against a life time self destructive habit: killing, smothering desire for what it is obvious I am not supposed to have, because I do not get it.

Isn't that exactly what I was told not to do?

So...a life lie would raise its head.

"Do not kill desire because you do not get what you desire." I whispered under my breath.

And so I allowed myself to actually taste the disappointment of not being able to do what I deeply wanted to do. And it actually hurt...deeply...in the depth of my spirit...and in an ironically healthy sort of way.

I was physically, mentally, and spiritually drained by the time we stopped for lunch.

An old man showed up and joined us for lunch where I was staying. And we got talking...actually the others talked...I was more or less a sponge.

Suffice to say heard from God and also got to cry loud and long and hard on a "stand in for a dad's" shoulder.

Several weeks later, I wrote the following in a blog.

I was warned it was coming...by an old man of God named Jim.

"God is going to take you on a little...side hike of sorts."

Gulp. Ok.

Several weeks later...

I do not even want to recall the confusing terrain of the last several weeks. I am becoming disillusioned by any "goodness" in the flesh (it may turn out Paul got that much right)...at the same time, I am being unstoppably overwhelmed by...Grace.

Take the last couple days, weeks, actually, when I fully expected to "get it" for frankly irrational behavior. And all I get is a sense of being held...

Held!!

By God.

Held...

Not scolded?

Held...

Not rebuked...

Held...

Not berated for bad performance?

Held...

As in, actually loved?

Held...

By a Father I hardly know and barely trust?

Held...
"It's okay"
(I know it's NOT ok)
Held...
I am not used to it
Held...
I am not sure I even like it
Held...
It is becoming clear that I need it
Held...
It confuses me
Held...
Ok...
I am slowly starting to get it.
Held...
This can only mean one thing.
Held...
This Father is unlike any other that I have known.
Held...
He is...not even angry.
In fact, He is...
Smiling?!
Held.
Long...Deep...Uncertain...Breath...
Held...
Unbelievable
Held...
Our eyes meet
Held...
He actually...
actually...
LIKES

me
?
Held...
I really don't know what to do with this.
Held...
But I kinda like it...
Held...

Would you like to see your manuscript become a book?

If you are interested in becoming a PublishAmerica author, please submit your manuscript for possible publication to us at:

acquisitions@publishamerica.com

You may also mail in your manuscript to:

**PublishAmerica
PO Box 151
Frederick, MD 21705**

We also offer free graphics for Children's Picture Books!

www.publishamerica.com

PublishAmerica

CPSIA information can be obtained at www.ICGtesting.com
Printed in the USA
BVOW071903231012

303750BV00001B/37/P